MARGARET HEBBLETHWAITE

Finding God In All Things

Praying with St Ignatius

T0111739

Collins
FOUNT PAPERBACKS

C 00234 3189

FLL88/14135   8/11
X/

248 ·32 HEB

First published in Great Britain
by Fount Paperbacks, London in 1987

Copyright © Margaret Hebblethwaite 1987

Made and printed in Great Britain by
William Collins Sons & Co. Ltd, Glasgow

Conditions of Sale
This book is sold subject to the condition
that it shall not, by way of trade or otherwise
be lent, re-sold, hired out or otherwise circulated
without the publisher's prior consent in any form of
binding or cover other than that in which it is
published and without a similar condition
including this condition being imposed
on the subsequent purchaser

Contents

Acknowledgements 8

Introduction: *Why Ignatius?* 9

1. *Using What Helps* 17

    Using creation 20
    Using the body in prayer 23
    Using our mental faculties 27
    Using every circumstance 29

2. *Avoiding What Hinders* 32

    Indifference 38
    Generosity 44

3. *Learning to Pray* 49

    Choosing a time 55
    Choosing a place 59

4. *Structuring a Prayer Time* 64

    Preparation 66
    Preparatory prayer 68
    The First Prelude: the history 69
    The Second Prelude: composition of place 70
    The Third Prelude: what I want 74
    Points 79

Colloquy   82
Closing   86
Appendix to Chapter 4: Some Prayers .   88

5. *Reading, Meditating, Praying*   91

   Texts from scripture   92
   Other texts   95
   Appendix to Chapter 5: Some texts
      for *lectio divina*   99

6. *Contemplating*   102

   Imaginative exercises not from scripture   106
   Imaginative contemplation of a gospel mystery 111
   Appendix to Chapter 6: Some contemplations   119

7. *Noticing What Happens*   130

   Reviewing one prayer period   132
   Repetition   137
   Reviewing a longer stretch   139

8. *Being Sorry*   143

   Penance   146
   Examination of conscience: evil in the world   149
   Examination of conscience: scripture   155
   Examination of conscience: check-lists   157
   Appendix to Chapter 8:
   Some forms of General Examen   161

9. *Loving Jesus*   167

    Infancy   168
    Ministry   169
    Passion and resurrection   170
    The preferential option for the poor   172

10. *Discerning*   177

    Consolation and desolation   183
    Dryness   189
    Distractions   192
    Deception   193

11. *Decision-making*   201

    The discernment process   206
    Some exercises   211
    Communal discernment   214
    An example   217

12. *Finding God in All Things*   222

    The final contemplation   224
    God's indwelling   228

Index to the *Spiritual Exercises*   233

General Index   237

Acknowledgements

The translation I have used of the *Spiritual Exercises* is generally that of Louis J. Puhl (Loyola University Press, Chicago, 1951), and I acknowledge with gratitude permission to quote from that text. I have made occasional adaptation to avoid sexist language, and sometimes I have used a more traditional term where it is more commonly known, eg "Three Degrees of Humility" for "Three Kinds of Humility". Numbers in brackets throughout the book are references to paragraphs in the *Spiritual Exercises*.

The translation of the "Take and Receive" prayer on p. 222 is from David L. Fleming's *A Contemporary Reading of the Spiritual Exercises* (Institute of Jesuit Sources, St Louis, Missouri, 1978).

Most quotations from the Bible are from the Revised Standard Version of the Bible, copyrighted 1946, 1952, © 1971, 1973 by the Division of Christian Education of the National Council of the Churches of Christ in the USA, and used by permission.

Introduction

Ignatian spirituality is undergoing a boom. Fifteen years ago few people had heard of it, unless, as a Jesuit or a Jesuit-dependent nun, they had been subjected to the old, haranguing "choose hell or heaven before lunch" style of retreat. Now lay people as much as religious and clergy, women as much as men, Anglicans and increasingly Free Church members as much as Roman Catholics, are talking Ignatian, reading Ignatian, and urging each other to make an Ignatian retreat. Why such a dramatic change? And what is Ignatian spirituality anyway?

Ignatius of Loyola (or Inigo, to give him his real, Spanish name) was an ambitious and extravagant sixteenth-century Spaniard, who began life in love with fighting, beautiful women and chivalry. A bishop of Salamanca gives us this vignette of the young Ignatius: "He was walking along a street up which came a group of men who jostled him and forced him against the wall. At once he whipped out his sword and gave after them to the end of the street. Had there not been passers-by to restrain him, he would surely have killed some of those men, or they would have killed him."

Ignatius' life changed when, at about thirty, he was caught in the siege of Pamplona, attacked by the French. It was evident to all that they were fighting a losing battle and should surrender before more lives were lost. But Ignatius, who was not the surrendering type, succeeded in persuading them that that would be cowardly. The fortress was bombarded and fell, and Ignatius got a cannonball through the leg. He had to have the leg set and reset, and he nearly died of the injury. He was compelled to lie in bed for some ten months, and limped for the rest of his days.

While he was convalescing his ambition began to take a different turn. He now began to dream of being Christ's knight, and of doing great deeds for the love of God. When he was able to walk again he went to a place of pilgrimage in the mountains called Montserrat. There he made a confession in writing of the sins of his whole life (it took him three days). Then he exchanged clothes with a poor man (who was afterwards charged with stealing them), and made a night vigil before the black Madonna of Montserrat. His new life had begun.

At first Ignatius was a begger and a hermit, then a pilgrim. Afterwards he began to study for the priesthood, and found during this time that some prayer exercises he had devised were very helpful to the other students. And so the famous Spiritual Exercises were born.

In the suspicious atmosphere of the Inquisition he was pressured to leave Spain, and completed his studies in Paris, where a group of fellow ordinands took vows with him in a private little ceremony at Montmartre in 1534. They became the first Companions, that is, the first members of the Company of Jesus, usually known in English as the Society of Jesus or the Jesuits. It is now far and away the largest male religious order in the world, with twenty-six thousand members.

Around the time that the Catholic Church as a whole was undergoing a renewal, in the period surrounding the Second Vatican Council, the Jesuits, like many other religious orders, were looking back to their origins and going through their own process of renewal. In particular they did much historical work on the Spiritual Exercises and the early traditions of giving them, and realized how far Jesuit practice had strayed from the original intention.

Where Ignatius had laid down individual direction, retreats had come to be given in large groups. Where Ignatius had decreed everyone should proceed at their own speed, as God led each individual, retreats had been rigidly programmed into ready-made slots. Where Ignatius had insisted that any points given by the director should be kept brief to allow the maximum of work to be done by the retreatant, the custom had grown up of giving preached retreats. Where Ignatius had given his direction to Jesuits and non-Jesuits alike, the Spiritual Exercise had come to be the reserve of a clerical élite.

There was need for a radical change of approach, a return to the beginnings, if the authentic Spiritual Exercises were to be experienced once more.

By the end of the 1970s this renewal of the Exercises had spread more or less throughout the world. It became normal once more for individual and daily direction to replace talks entirely in the full Exercises (known as the "thirty-day retreat" or the "long retreat"). Shorter, "eight-day" retreats followed a similar method. The practice of discernment (for which see Chapters 10 and 11) became understood and practised once more.

And, most importantly, the Jesuits once more began to share their heritage with the rest of the Church: retreat houses opened their doors to all; many Sisters from Ignatian-based orders stopped being passive listeners and were allowed to give the Spiritual Exercises themselves; and on their heels came the laity and members of other churches. More and more people were helped to develop a prayer life through the ideas of Ignatius, which became a leaven in the Church.

The international network of the religious orders enabled this change to take place around the world very quickly. In Great Britain a decisive step forward was made by St Beuno's retreat house in North Wales, which the Jesuits Michael Ivens and Gerard Hughes (author of *God of Surprises*) pioneered,

11

though several other retreat houses now offer similar opportunities, and a network of Ignatian-trained spiritual directors is webbing out all over Britain.

Even people who have not yet caught up with Ignatian spirituality have mostly heard of Jesuits. The old image of the English Jesuit was of a tall, severe man in a black gown, with wings. The new image of the Latin American Jesuit is of a bearded hero in a remote jungle hide-out. (Jeremy Irons' brilliant portrayal of Father Gabriel in the film *The Mission* has given this image wider circulation, but there are many such working in the poorest areas of Latin America today.) Though these pictures seem very different, what they have in common is something of the totality of an Ignatius, who could pray like this (and if it is not his prayer, as tradition holds, it is an authentic reflection of his thinking).

> Lord, teach me to be generous.
> Teach me to serve you as you deserve;
> to give and not to count the cost,
> to fight and not to heed the wounds,
> to toil and not to seek for rest,
> to labour and not to ask for any reward
> save that of knowing that I do your holy will.

This book is not about Jesuits, nor even about Ignatius, and it is important to say that because the last thing Ignatian spirituality is about is turning everyone into a Jesuit, or holding up Ignatius' life as a model to copy. That would be a complete misunderstanding, for Ignatian spirituality is rather about discovering the unique person that each of us is, the individual ways in which each of us relates to God, and the unprescribable ways in which we are each called to do God's will.

In other words it is not a "rule", and those formed by

Ignatian spirituality are in no way members of a "third order". As a layperson, proud of the freedom and variety of the lay life, I have always maintained Ignatian spirituality is the ideal approach for us, because everything is individually tailored, and there is no fitting square pegs into round holes.

The reason why I have begun with Ignatius and Jesuits is rather to give some idea of context: Ignatian spirituality has not sprung out of the air in the 1980s, nor are the ideas I write of my own.

The Ignatian school of prayer is rich and comprehensive because it teaches not so much by giving a method as by helping people notice what the Spirit is doing in them, and the ways in which the Spirit works are as manifold as creation itself. There is nothing God has made that cannot be used to speak to us of God and to lead us to God; if we want to explore the length and breadth, the depth and height of God's love, then we must look all around us, for creation is full of it.

"The world is charged with the grandeur of God", said Gerard Manley Hopkins, the Jesuit poet, and that does not apply only to nature but to every human experience. We can find a way to God whether we experience joy or pain, loss or gain, the everyday or the extraordinary. "Finding God in all things" – the title of this book – is one of the phrases most associated with Ignatian spirituality, and it refers in a special way to the peak of the Exercises – the *Contemplatio ad Amorem* – which is the subject of the last chapter.

How this works out in terms of teaching people to pray, can be illustrated in a few examples. Where another school of prayer might give you one position for prayer (for example, "When you pray, sit with a straight back"), Ignatius will talk of sitting, standing, walking, kneeling, lying, or anything else that is helping you at this particular time.

Where another school of prayer might give you one technique (for example, saying your mantra over and over),

Ignatian spirituality covers so many methods that almost anything that anyone has ever thought of as prayer can be found in the Spiritual Exercises in some form or another, and certainly no method of meditation already practised will be rejected.

Where another school of prayer might promise you one result (for example, peace of heart), Ignatius explicitly recognizes so much of the varied and confusing responses people can have – anywhere on the spectrum of what he calls consolation, desolation and dryness – that no one need ever feel they are having the wrong reactions or that the method does not work for them. Yet along with all this variety goes a readily grasped practicality. The Ignatian school believes that prayer can be taught, and that is something very comforting. There is no point in exhorting people to pray if you do not tell them how. Contemplation, meditation and the like are not obscure gifts to the select few, but something that anyone can learn, that anyone can be taught, and that do not lose their wonder and graciousness for all that.

Instead of propounding sublime ideals of what prayer is, so that you feel inadequate and do not know where to begin, Ignatian spirituality very practically tells you what to do. And when you have done it, it tells you what to do next. And if the suggestion does not feel right, but something else does, then it tells you to follow the something else, because it is not Ignatius who is running your prayer life but God.

Now this is where a book has to be an inadequate reflection of Ignatius' teaching, because the real spiritual direction can only be done on a one-to-one basis. And that applies no less to Ignatius' own book, the *Spiritual Exercises*. It is not a book to be read, and I do not recommend reading it. As one Jesuit friend said to me, "I am glad to say it is rather hard to get hold of copies." I have included a text at the start of each chapter, and I quote from it freely throughout, but then I can explain anything puzzling or off-putting as I go.

The *Spiritual Exercises* is a handbook for retreat-givers who

14

have already had the experience of making their own Exercises under another's direction, and so can relate to what is being talked about. People who give the Exercises refer constantly back to the book – there is no question of getting away from the text, but only of understanding what Ignatius is really on about, seen across the gap of centuries. At the end of this book is an index to the *Spiritual Exercises* which shows all the paragraphs of Ignatius to which I have referred. Everything I say is there in the *Spiritual Exercises* somewhere, if you know where to look, or is what I hope is a legitimate extension of Ignatius. Throughout the book I give numbers in brackets which are references to paragraphs in the *Spiritual Exercises*.

This book tries to be a mediation and an explanation of some key Ignatian ideas. It does not try to be a do-it-yourself retreat, but it does suggest some prayer exercises that can be done as well outside of retreat as in. If you want to have the real experience of the Spiritual Exercises then you will need to find a spiritual director.

But there are many ways in which Ignatian spirituality can illumine our lives outside of the intense retreat experience, and this book is for those times. It is intended as an introduction for those who know nothing of Ignatian spirituality but are interested, but it is also for those who know and love Ignatian ideas and would like to explore them further. Perhaps most of all it is for people who do not much care if an idea is labelled "Ignatian" or not, but simply want to go further in their relationship with God.

I try to be faithful to Ignatius' intentions, but what I say will inevitably be limited by the extent of my understanding. So, *in so far as I have understood Ignatius*, this is what he is saying. . . .

HAMMERSMITH & FULHAM PUBLIC LIBRARIES

1

Using What Helps

The other things on the face of the earth are created for us to help us in attaining the end for which we are created. Hence we are to make use of them in as far as they help us in the attainment of our end. . . .

Our one desire and choice should be what is more conducive to the end for which we are created. (23)

A book on prayer could properly begin by asking why we should pray anyway. But before we can answer the question "Why pray?" we ought to ask the question "Why anything?" Why should we do anything at all? What is it all for anyway? What is the purpose of life?

It may be that we do not know, and if that is the case I have always felt that committing suicide was a very rational thing to do; unless, like the French writer Pascal, we think we should behave as though there is a God, just to be on the safe side in case there is one after all. But it is unlikely that many people will have decided to read this book, which has God in the title, unless they have some sort of religious faith. So I will take it as an assumption that we believe we are created by God. There are different ways in which such a believer in God can articulate an answer to the question: "What is the purpose of life?" They all amount to much the same, though they may use different words and have a slightly different feel to them.

The prayer Ignatius placed at the beginning of the Spiritual Exercises (the "Soul of Christ", see Appendix to Chapter 4) sees the end of our existence as "that with your saints I may praise you for ever and ever".

So the little red "penny" catechism on which all good Catholics were brought up twenty years ago put it this way:

2. Why did God make you?

God made me to know him, love him and serve him in this world, and to be happy with him for ever in the next.

Not everyone is comfortable talking about the saints or the next world, but most people love the classic statement of life's meaning by St Augustine, which really says the same thing, but more powerfully:

The thought of you stirs us so deeply that we cannot be content unless we praise you, because you have made us for yourself and our hearts find no peace until they rest in you.

(Confessions, 1, 1)

In short, the end of our life is God, and the task of our life is to find the way to God. That is not one purpose among many, but the sole and over-riding aim of all existence.

This may seem rather obvious, but in practice we forget it, and behave as though the purpose of life was security, or money, or comfort, or status. Few people, even among good Christians, seem to mind admitting that they took a new job because it was a promotion, or because it was better paid. We hardly ever hear anyone give as their reason that they thought it would help them come closer to God, or that they felt it was what God was asking of them. And yet that should be the only reason why we ever do anything.

The point of praying is to bring us back into remembrance of the truth that we are made for God. It is to strengthen and reaffirm our commitment to God as the purpose of our life, and the end of our days. It is to remember what we are about, so that the rest of our lives may be more ordered to that purpose.

Ignatius said that every time we pray we should begin with recalling that end. He called it the "preparatory prayer" (46, 49), or the "First Principle and Foundation" (23). It is really the fundamental attitude of prayer itself – to ask for the grace that everything I do or intend should be directed purely to the praise and service of God. And, moving from prayer into the choices of life, Ignatius is constantly reminding us that our decisions should be based on what is more for the glory and praise of God and our own eternal salvation (179).

Here is how one modern preacher explained this purpose of prayer:

Let us take the prayer of Jesus. For John, to know who Jesus is is to know that he comes from the Father and he goes to the Father. Coming from the Father and going to him is not just something accidental to Jesus. It is not, so to speak, a journey that Jesus happens to make. It means that he is the one who receives all that is from the Father, whose whole being is a gift from the Father, and whose whole life is ordered to the Father. He is the Father's Word. And so for Jesus to pray to the Father is simply for him to show who he is.

Now when we pray, we also disclose, in a sense, who we are. In Christ we are from the Father and for the Father. God is our Alpha and our Omega, our beginning and our end. We may define ourselves by all sorts of little projects, and intentions, whether to gain wealth or reputation or have lots of children, but in prayer we disclose who we really are, and what it means for us to be human; we disclose our ultimate end. We are those who find ourselves between a birth we cannot remember and a death that we would rather forget. And when we pray, we disclose, to ourselves and to others, who we are, where we come from and where we are going, that we are from God and for God.

We may know intellectually, we may know in theory that we are going to die, that we are mortal. But any knowledge is only real and true if it finds expression. We may know in principle, in theory, that God is the source of everything; we may know in theory that everything is a gift from him. But unless we celebrate this fact, express it, bring it to word and gesture, then the sense will atrophy. We need to pray so that we will not forget who we are, and where we are going to.

(Timothy Radcliffe, OP, 7th Sunday of Easter, 1984)

Using creation

The purpose of life is to make our way to God, and we pray so that we will not forget. All creation, everything God has made, has this finality: it is made by God and put at our service. And so, points out Ignatius, rather obviously:

> The other things on the face of the earth are created for us to help us in attaining the end for which we are created. Hence, we are to make use of them in as far as they help us in the attainment of our end. (23)

Many things that are obvious, however, do not sink in. The point to be spelled out here, is that creation is not intended to be some kind of rival to God, but rather an assistance towards God. So that we are not asked to choose *between* God and the world, but rather to enjoy God *through* the world, and to find God in all things. All that is good speaks to us of God, and we should let these good things speak loudly, not quell their voices as though the God we worship was one of miserable abnegation.

Many Christians have thought in the past that if something was enjoyable they must have none of it. Sex was a powerful force, so it must be denied. Human love brought fearsome risks. Drink was dubious (the turning of water into wine at the marriage of Cana was quietly forgotten, along with the charge that Jesus behaved like a glutton and a drunkard – Luke 7:34). Funfairs, dances and the theatre were regarded with suspicion. And the God we were left with was really rather dull. Nor did he bear much family resemblance to Jesus' Father. We have only to think of the dreary greys and browns of the Puritans, or the way Catholic nuns were taught to behave twenty years ago – never going out unless in pairs, always wearing lace-up shoes – to remember what a hold this jealous, gloomy God has had on us.

Such is not the God of Ignatius, nor of any of the real saints. We are called, not to diminishment, but to exploration. We are invited to *use* the world, for that is why it has been given us. Things other than God have been made to help us in the search for God; they should be used, and can be used, for that purpose. Some people talk of this attitude to the world, as "creation-centred spirituality".

Probably the most powerful experience most people have had in their lives is the experience of human love. Whether it is painful and frustrated, or happy and fulfilled, it is potentially a privileged path to God, because God is love. A twentieth-century writer called Ida Coudenhove had this to say about finding God in the most overwhelming experiences of human love:

But we prefer to twist the truth awry, to calumniate and abuse the love given to men and women for each other, and are ashamed of it because it so often makes God's victory difficult – instead of seeing that the evil does not consist in its strength, that may be the best thing about us in God's eyes, even now, but in the feebleness of our love to God, due to very different reasons. The man without the love of God has indeed good cause to worry about the threat to his salvation in "earthly" love: for it is a reality, and where it finds unclaimed territory it takes possession. Did we, however, love God, really love him, then we should have no need to draw narrow boundaries round our love for his creatures, we could throw ourselves boldly into the sea and let the tide sweep us away, praying for the increase, not the death, of our love.

And I maintain that the way to Divine Love is not spiritual self-mutilation, however many weighty opinions declare it to be so, but that the gift of human love is a mirror, which though dim and broken, is still the plainest in which to see what our love to God might be; the alphabet from which, like children learning to read, we spell out the language we should speak to God.

There is, of course, disordered love, but there is not a "good" and a "bad" love. There is only good love.

(*Essays in Order*, Sheed and Ward, London, 1932, pp. 80–1)

If God is love, then let our love speak to us of God. If God is good, then let what is good speak to us of God. If God is joy, then let what fills us with joy speak to us of God. If God is peace, then let what brings us peace speak to us of God. If God is life, then let what is full of life speak to us of God.

I have come
so that they may have life,
and have it to the full. (John 10:10)

22

We do not need to be fearful and mistrustful of the dangers of the surrounding world, for

> Anyone who enters through me will be safe:
> such a one will go in and out
> and will find pasture. (John 10:9)

If we approach the world with such confident freedom, so too should we approach prayer. Praying is not some tight exercise, with sore knees and a bad back, fingers pushed hard against each other, eyes screwed up, mind ticking rigorously through a prescribed course. Prayer is an exploration of all our faculties as channels towards God, and we will not explore very far unless we wander and experiment and stretch ourselves.

Using the body in prayer

Even in bodily terms there is great scope and much to be discovered. As already mentioned (p. 13), Ignatius suggests a variety of physical positions, and the principle is to use what is most effective (76). Often sitting is the best posture, because it is restful, and we can devote our attention more fully to our prayer without unnecessary distractions from physical discomfort. There is no need to feel irreverent about praying in a sitting position – even for sacred moments like those after receiving communion – if we can pray better that way and be more wholly engrossed in God.

Still more restful is lying on our back. If it helps the prayer, use it; if it sends us to sleep, we defeat our aim. If kneeling makes us aware of God's holiness and keeps our attention fixed, it is a good position. If lying prostrate on our face expresses something powerful for us, we should not be embarrassed to be so demonstrative, at least in private. If standing expresses our respect and readiness to do God's will, then stand. But do not bob up and down trying everything in turn; Ignatius tells us to maintain the same position so long as we continue to find what we desire there, in other words, so long as it remains helpful.

There are a number of prayer exercises that concentrate particularly on what we are doing with our bodies, and these are more fully explained in the modern classic, *Sadhana*, by the late Indian Jesuit Anthony de Mello (Gujarat Sahitya Prakash, Anand, India, 1978), who has been greatly influenced by Hindu and Buddhist methods of meditation. Pure bodily awareness has unexpected potentialities for bringing us into an awareness of God.

For example, we can sit cross-legged, with our back straight, our eyes closed and our hands resting in our lap, facing upwards, and then simply become aware of all the sensations in, say, our right hand. As we remain quietly concentrated on this, we will become aware of many feelings that usually remain dormant until we focus our attention on them. This simple act of awareness brings us into communion with the God who gives life at every moment to every nerve of our body.

Another exercise of bodily awareness is concentrated on our breathing. We do not do anything different with our breathing, but simply become aware of it. We feel the air coming into our nostrils; and we feel the air going out again. We can think at the same time of the Holy Spirit as the breath of life. If we want, we can make the breath in a prayer for God to fill us, and the breath out a prayer for purification.

Another awareness exercise, focused on a different sense, is to listen for all the tiny noises that we can hear in a place that we usually think of as quiet, or silent. Soon we will be hearing distant cars, and birdsong, and wind, and maybe even sounds from within our own heads. "Be still and know that I am God" (Psalm 46:10).

Simple awareness exercises like these can fill an entire prayer period. Or they can be used as preparatory for another meditation, for example, praying on scripture or examining our conscience. Any exercise like this that quietens and stills us in the presence of God can be known as "centring prayer": it is the beginning of the quiet that lets us enter the depths of our own being, where God is hidden.

There are other exercises that use the body, besides pure awareness. Again, *Sadhana* is the best source for these.

We can (in private, or we will feel inhibited) speak with our body to God. We can say, "I offer myself to you". How would I say that, with my body? We can say, "I am sorry". How could I say that? Or how would I say, "I worship you"? There is value in taking this slowly, and in letting the gestures be as total as possible – arms stretched right out, face tilted right back, nothing half-given or half-said, praying the same gesture over again, for "as often as you find devotion in performing it", says Anthony de Mello, on firm Ignatian principles.

There are already traditional gestures for some of these prayers: we can use them, if they fit for us, instead of making new ones. There is beating the breast with the fist, for example, for repentance. Or genuflection, for adoration. There is making the sign of the cross, for asking God to be with us. There is kissing the crucifix, for humbly thanking Christ for his saving passion. There is stretching out the arms in a kneeling position, for beseeching God with great fervour and self-offering. There is bowing before God, in a standing position, for showing reverence. And so on.

If we make up new gestures, and begin to feel at ease in this form of expression, we can try going through a short prayer (the Our Father, for example) and praying each phrase with our body. We are beginning to build up a meditative dance. David danced before the Lord with all his might (2 Samuel

6:14). There is an Eastern meditative dance called *T'ai Chi Ch'uan*, which is slow and controlled and takes about a quarter of an hour. Dancing before God is prayer, if we choose to make it so.

I am still talking here about what we do in our private devotions. Dancing before God in the liturgy serves a different purpose – the edification of the community rather than the self-expression of the individual – and it needs to be well done. But in our personal prayer we need not worry what we look like.

Yet we may not choose to do anything so extravagant or imaginative in our prayer, but simply, in the most quiet and minimal way, find a composed and reverent position, with a straight spine, that we can maintain without discomfort. Even so we might find Ignatius' suggestion helpful, that we make a physical act of entering into our chosen place of prayer, rather as Moses took off his shoes before the presence of God in the burning bush:

> I will stand for the space of an *Our Father*, a step or two before the place where I am to meditate or contemplate, and with my mind raised on high, consider that God our Lord beholds me, etc. Then I will make an act of reverence or humility. (75)

To mark the beginning of our meditation physically like this can help us to enter more decisively and deeply into prayer, and in a comparable way we can mark the end (I use the sign of the cross), so that we are not drifting in and out, but are giving ourselves to it more fully. There is a time for drifting in and out of prayer, but that is something different from a period set aside for God.

Even in the simplest ways like this, without doing anything fancy, we are following the injunction of Paul: "present your bodies as a living sacrifice, holy and acceptable to God, which is your spiritual worship" (Romans 12:1). When we find ourselves, in prayer, so useless that we feel we are not doing anything at all, the mere fact of choosing to be bodily present to God is itself our prayer, and a good one: the Jesuit Edward Yarnold, who runs our retreat team in Oxford, says that when we feel we can do nothing else we can at least ask to be like one of the statues in God's church, worshipping God by doing nothing else but being there.

Using our mental faculties

As we try to make use of anything in creation that can lead us to God, there is a great deal we can make use of in our prayer apart from our bodies. More will be said in Chapter 4 about the different ways in which a prayer period can be subdivided to make fuller use of the different tools of prayer open to us. One of our faculties, the imagination, is so rich in its potential for prayer, and its use is so distinctive of Ignatian method, that I shall be devoting Chapter 6 to it. There is a great deal more to lift prayer out of the confines of a "saying set prayers" approach, and to let it stretch into the corners of our being.

It is not that prayer is no good unless it feels rich and fulfilling, for sometimes God chooses to give us dry prayer; it is rather that God expects us to do our bit, to make use of the available possibilities and our God-given faculties, because "the other things on the face of the earth are created for us to help us in attaining the end for which we are created". If we do our bit, then we can let come what will come, according to God's will.

Ignatius found it useful sometimes to separate out different faculties in our prayer, and would distinguish praying with the intellect, for example, from praying with the core of the self – what was called in those days the "will". (3). With the intellect we reason, and so this kind of prayer can be called, in quite ordinary language, thinking.

Sometimes, instead, Ignatius makes a threefold division and speaks of the three powers of the soul: we can pray with our memory, with our understanding and with our will (45,50). Memory and understanding are both forms of thinking, but while memory recalls the story we are praying over, understanding reflects on it in more detail. With the will we "manifest our love", and here he is referring to the way we gather up our thoughts to ask something of God, or thank God for something, or express our sorrow at something, or praise God for something, or simply send a willed wave of love towards God. It is more obvious that these are prayer than that the more wandering thoughts are prayer, and Ignatius acknowledges that praying with the will calls for greater reverence than praying with the intellect.

At the risk of sounding over-complicated, it is normal to use our will more at the beginning and end of prayer: at the beginning in that act of choice when we decide to enter into prayer, and at the end when we draw the threads together to express something to God before saying goodbye. These acts of will, as it were, embrace our prayer and consecrate the whole period to God, even if we have been distracted and scattered in the meantime.

Some people whose chief model of prayer is saying prayers do not immediately realize that quietly thinking about the mysteries of our faith, and having ideas and reflections on them, can form a large part of prayer as well as the things we choose to say to God. Having thoughts is not just food for prayer, but can be an actual part of the prayer. Many of the thoughts that come into our mind will be given by God, so we should let them come with a relaxed and receptive spirit. As Ignatius says so simply when talking of prayer before the crucified Christ, "I shall ponder upon what presents itself to my mind" (53).

Other people find it hard to consider thinking a form of prayer for another reason: they have read in mystical literature that we must empty our mind, and banish all thoughts and images. Any thought then, however holy, appears to them invalid as true contemplation. In this way many of the Holy Spirit's gifts are booted out of the window again, and the net result may be that we find our attempts to pray such a boring and frustrating effort that we soon discontinue them.

Ignatius had a much broader understanding of prayer than this. There is certainly a time for the centring-prayer methods of stilling, quietening and focusing; there are times too when the sort of prayer God gives us is the rather empty experience known as the prayer of quiet; but that does not mean that kind of gift from God is the only one we should accept in prayer. We have to remember that it is not us, nor even Ignatius, who is running our prayer life, but God.

Using every circumstance

When we say that anything can be used to bring us to God, that applies not only to the splendid, rich opportunities, but the poor and weak ones too. God can make use of whatever our circumstances are. We find God by exploring to the ends of the earth, but we can also find God when confined to a narrow prison. We can find God by becoming a mother, or we can find God by becoming a nun. We can find God by reading a holy book, or we can find God by reading the newspaper. It depends rather on whether we are looking for God, than on whether we have the right opportunities. We can find God in all things.

We may ideally prefer to pray before a beautiful sunset over the sea, in a warm climate, with the sound of crickets gently lulling us into communion with God. But if where we happen to be is an underheated house in a noisy street in a dirty slum then that is no excuse for not praying, nor any reason why our prayer will be less effective. We may ideally prefer to make a retreat in an isolated retreat house with lots of silence and no everyday concerns to occupy us – and indeed, Ignatius says, we should so choose if we can (20) – but if we cannot, then God can use what opportunities we have, not just as a second-best, but as the providential circumstances for us here and now. God can make use of anything. If we give with generosity all that is possible, God will do the rest.

One standard example of this principle is what is known as Ignatius' "19th Annotation" (number 19 of the notes at the beginning of the Spiritual Exercises). This says that the Spiritual Exercises can be done not only by those with the time and leisure to take a month doing nothing else; they can also be made by those who simply cannot leave the rest of their lives behind for so long. It may be a matter of "public affairs", or it may be another kind of "necessary business", from having small children at home to being engaged in a course of studies or under contract to an employer. Many people who are tied down like this can still benefit greatly from doing Ignatius' Exercises, which should then be given more slowly over a longer period of time.

In the recent renewal of Ignatian practice, many such "19th Annotation" retreats have been made in the course of daily life. They can last from a few weeks to many months, and usually involve doing one exercise a day, and seeing a spiritual director about once a week. It is a practice that is spreading fast, especially among lay people, but it does depend on finding a director. This book cannot be used to make such a retreat, though it can serve as a preparation, or as a refresher on Ignatian ideas afterwards.

And so, while we should always do all we can to give to God good things – a good time, a good place, a good preparation, a good position, and everything else good that we can offer in so far as lies in our power – in the end all is grace. We do not control good prayer by our preparations, but only dispose ourselves for it. God does the rest.

2

Avoiding What Hinders

The other things on the face of the earth are created for us to help us in attaining the end for which we are created. Hence . . . we must rid ourselves of them in as far as they prove a hindrance to us.

Therefore, we must make ourselves indifferent to all created things, as far as we are allowed free choice and are not under any prohibition. Consequently, as far as we are concerned, we should not prefer health to sickness, riches to poverty, honour to dishonour, a long life to a short life. The same holds for all other things.

Our one desire and choice should be what is more conducive to the end for which we are created. (23)

There must be a catch somewhere to all the permissiveness of the last chapter, and here it is. On the one hand, if things help us to God, we should use them; but on the other, if they get in the way, we should leave them aside. This is where discipline, self-control and mortification come in. All things *can* help, but not all things *do* help, at least not all the time.

Ignatius, of course, is not the only person to have had such an insight. Every great spiritual teacher has said the same. What Ignatius does, as I have said before and no doubt will say again, is not to give us a new teaching, but to dwell on and draw out the implications of what we already know but tend to ignore; and he invites us to do the same – to let truths sink in, by praying on them.

Ignatius' principle of "use things in as far as they help, avoid things in as far as they hinder" is captured in almost identical words in a little prayer by St Nicholas Flue:

Lord, grant me everything that helps me on the way to you;
Lord, take away from me everything that hinders me on
the way to you.

Or we can take an example, in more extravagant language,
from the passionate fourteenth-century English hermit,
Richard Rolle:

> If it is for God's sake that we love everything, we love God
> in it rather than the thing itself. And so we rejoice, not in it
> but in God – in whom, indeed, we shall glory and rejoice
> for ever. But evil people are out to enjoy this present world,
> and they make it the object of their love: they are always
> seeking things to do with worldly pleasure. What greater
> folly, more pitiful and damning, can anyone show than to
> cling to things which are by their very nature passing and
> decaying? For God the Holy Trinity is to be loved for
> himself alone.

(The Fire of Love, 4)

But my favourite passage, as usual comes from Augustine,
where he describes how the good things of creation, that
could – and should – have pointed him to God, diverted him
instead, by becoming ends in themselves:

> Late, late have I loved you, Beauty at once so ancient and
> so new! Late have I loved you! You were within me, and I
> was in the world outside myself. I searched for you outside
> myself and, disfigured as I was, I fell upon the lovely things
> of your creation. You were with me, but I was not with you.
> The beautiful things of this world kept me far from you
> and yet, if they had not been in you, they would have had
> no being at all.

(Confessions X,27)

"The beautiful things of this world kept me far from you." We all have some experience of over-indulging in good things that then become bad for us and make us unhappy. It may be an inclination to drink too much, or to smoke, or to eat more than we intend; it may be a laziness about planning our finances so as to be able to pay our bills; it may be an inability to end a relationship that is causing us a lot of unnecessary pain; it may be a habit of going to bed too late so that getting up in the morning is an agony. Immediate desire wins out over longer-term well-being, again and again. Sometimes the situation has to become critical before we are spurred to take the quite simple steps of self-discipline that will make us feel better.

What Augustine and Ignatius invite us to do is to look not just at those middle-term ends of health and happiness but at our final end of closeness to God. They invite us to notice what is happening to us in the choices we make, and to ask ourselves about every decision, "Is this bringing me closer to God, or taking me away?"

In the end it is only common sense to sift out the acts that deepen our relationship with God, and to leave behind those that make us forget God. But although it is common sense it requires a conscious act of regular self-awareness, that we are often too lazy to make. We prefer to muddle along satisfying our immediate wants, rather than to take an overview of the general direction of our lives.

This conscious act of regular self-awareness is what Ignatius calls examination of conscience, or review. We tend to call it examination of conscience when we look at what we have done in our daily life, and review when we look at what we have done in our times of prayer. But the principle is the same: we recall what we did then, we notice how we feel about it now, and in the light of that we may adjust our plans for next time. Review will be described in more detail in Chapter 7, examination of conscience in Chapter 8.

There is a very important point in all this that needs spelling out, and it is a very Ignatian point. We are, to a large extent, and particularly, alas, as Christians, brought up on rules: these things are good, those things are bad. But such rules can only be a crude attempt to systematize what Ignatius sums up as one single and fundamental principle (in other words, his First Principle and Foundation): our end is God; therefore what helps towards God is good, what gets in the way is bad. Things are not good or bad in themselves, but only in the effect they have on our relationship with God. We can recall Augustine's classic, rule-defying pronouncement: "Love, and do what you will."

The "things of this world" that kept Augustine from God were not necessarily bad things; on the contrary, they were "beautiful things", things which could and should have reminded Augustine of the one without whom "they would have had no being at all". But they had become hindrances, because he forgot that. They needed to be got out of the way, so that he could see the one behind them. The task is not to refer to some list to see whether something is good or bad, but to ask ourselves in each individual instance, "Is this getting in the way of my relationship with God?"

This approach is a radical break-through from the way many of us have been brought up, at the same time less constrictive and more demanding.

Catholics of my generation and older were given a regime of what was sufficient to be a good Catholic. It was all laid out in the little, red "penny" catechism: there were the Commandments of God (the ten commandments) and then there were the Commandments of the Church (like going to mass on Sundays and holidays of obligation; and abstaining from meat on Fridays – the two practices that most marked out Catholics). Much confessional matter centred on violations of these rules. If you had said that although you had eaten fish on Friday you had not found God in the practice, the priest would have thought you perverse.

Inner attitudes were difficult to quantify; at least with external observances you knew what you were talking about. Of course some people looked for more than the sufficient: there have always been people who are serious about seeking holiness. But on the whole if you were looking for something more, the obvious choice would be to become a priest or a nun.

Lay people today are drawn to Ignatian spirituality when they are looking for that "something more". And the very word "more", in its Latin translation *magis*, is almost a technical term: what I desire, says Ignatius, is

> to choose what is *more* for the glory of His Divine Majesty and the salvation of my soul. (152, my italics)

Ignatius was, after all, an ambitious man, we remember, even though, in time, he turned his ambition into ambition for God. And Mary Ward, who more than anyone else was his female counterpart, had much the same approach to ambition. (She tried to found a women's equivalent of the Jesuits, in the early seventeenth century, and was imprisoned in the attempt as a "heretic, schismatic and rebel to Holy Church", but that is another story.) She said: "Timid persons will never ascend very high in the path of virtue, nor work anything great in the religious state." (*Till God Will*, p. 56, ed. M. Emmanuel Orchard, Darton, Longman and Todd, London, 1985)

It was, of course, much harder for women to be ambitious than men, as Mary Ward acknowledges:

> Wherein are we so inferior to other creatures that they should term us "but women"? As if we were in all things

36

inferior to some other creation, which I suppose to be men! Which, I dare be bold to say, is a lie and, with respect to the good Father, may say it is an error. I would to God that all men understood this verity, that women, if they will, may be perfect, and if they would not make us believe we can do nothing and that we are "but women", we might do great matters.

(ibid., pp. 57–8)

The difference between the "sufficient" approach and the desire for "more" is captured by Ignatius in what he calls the First and Second Degrees of Humility (165–6).

The First Degree of Humility, which is necessary (and, presumably, sufficient) for salvation, is based on obeying the law of God, in such a way that not for anything in the world "would I consent to violate a commandment, whether divine or human, that binds me under pain of mortal sin". This is very reminiscent of the spirituality recommended to Catholic laity thirty years ago.

But the Second Degree of Humility is not based on rule-keeping but on searching for the most God-directed option in every choice of our lives. The sins that concern us now are not the obvious and major law-breakings, but every shade of choice that reflects a desire for something other than the service of God. "Not for all creation, nor to save my life, would I consent to commit a venial sin." (166)

In the Third Degree of Humility Ignatius moves right beyond the language of avoiding sin, but that is for another chapter (see pp. 173).

The radical simplicity and challenge of the First Principle and Foundation is really for mature people. It allows a degree of freedom that not everyone can handle, and Ignatius warns that many people will not be ready to go on and tackle the full Spiritual Exercises, based as they are on developing this sense of individual discernment. It is not a matter of holiness attained, so much as of potentiality. Those who lack the maturity, or simply the intelligence, to grasp what is talked of or to cope with the responsibility that is given, are taught a much more rule-based approach – the Commandments, the Capital Sins, the precepts of the Church and the Works of Mercy (18).

Indifference

But even the most mature people are not immune from self-deception. If anything that helps me towards God is good, then all I have to do is convince myself that everything I want is helping me towards God. Then I can do exactly as I please.

Ignatius was by no means unaware of this danger. One of his Exercises (called the Three Classes of Person) tells the parable of someone who has acquired ten thousand ducats, and who, at the same time, wants to find peace in God by being spiritually detached from the money. There are different ways people have of kidding themselves in such a situation, but one typical variation is that of the Second Class of Person:

> They want to rid themselves of the attachment, but they wish to do so in such a way that they retain what they have acquired, so that God is to come to what they desire. (154)

And so, no sooner has Ignatius outlined the principle of "use what helps, avoid what hinders" in his First Principle and Foundation, than he goes straight on to talk about what he calls "indifference", which is the same as the less confusing term "detachment".

> Therefore, we must make ourselves indifferent to all created things . . . We should not prefer health to sickness, riches to poverty, honour to dishonour, a long life to a short life. The same holds for all other things. (23)

At this point one could say Ignatius had gone off his head. Of course we would all rather be healthy than sick, rich than poor, respected than despised, stay alive for longer rather than die now. If anyone thinks they have reached a state of mind when it does not matter to them, one could say, they are either deluding themselves, or suffering from masochism.

And yet "indifference", or "detachment", is so central to Ignatian spirituality that the entire Spiritual Exercises

> have as their purpose the conquest of self and the regulation of one's life in such a way that no decision is made under the influence of any inordinate attachment. (21)

In any case, Ignatius' logic cannot be faulted. Do we agree that we are made for God, who is the total fulfilment of all our ultimate longings? Do we agree that some things can move us towards that end, and others can send us further away from it? Then what is the point of having health but no God, or riches but no God, or honour but no God, or a long life but no God at the end of it?

I suppose we would agree with that, if we had to choose, but something in us wants to insist on having both – God *and* health, God *and* riches, God *and* honour, God *and* long life – just as the Second Class of Person wants to have God *and* the ten thousand ducats.

But God is so infinitely much more than these other things that in the end the "and" bit does not add anything. All that is good and that belongs to our eternal joy is included in God, for God is all in all. A beautiful expression of this finding of all we have loved and lost in our union with God, comes at the end of Francis' Thompson's famous poem, *The Hound of Heaven*:

All which I took from thee I did but take,
    Not for thy harms,
But just that thou might'st seek it in My arms.
    All which thy child's mistake
Fancies as lost, I have stored for thee at home:
    Rise, clasp My hand, and come!

Furthermore, we are not going to achieve much objectivity about what is and is not uniting us to God unless we have some measure of detachment from our other desires. To make a good and correct choice, Ignatius says,

> I should be like a balance at equilibrium, without leaning to either side, that I might be ready to follow whatever I perceive is more for the glory and praise of God our Lord and for the salvation of my soul. (179)

I said "some measure of detachment", for it is a misunderstanding to think Ignatius is suggesting we can turn ourselves into flat, feelingless zombies who do not suffer when we are sick, poor, despised or dying. That is not the point at all, and certainly Jesus, when he became human for us, suffered in such circumstances. It would even be heretical to say that he did not.

The point is not to deny that we have these desires, but to take them into account in such a way that we can achieve some measure of objectivity over and above them – so that we do not make choices that are based on them. That is what Ignatius means by the word "prefer" – not that we do not have such feelings, but that we choose not to base our decisions on their influence.

The most effective counter-balance to one want is to want something else even more; the most important counter-balance to our worldly desires is to desire God above all else.

The more our love of God grows, the less the other things seem to matter. The more we long for the total fulfilment that can be found in God alone, the less we mind about the partial fulfilments that satisfy only a part of our being. They will begin to assume a proportionate place when we see them in relation to the overall direction of our life, as possible staging posts on the journey to God, and that is just what the First Principle and Foundation is all about.

If we can see that even in unemployment we are learning something about valuing people for themselves rather than their labels, if even in bereavement we are learning something about the tenacity of true love, if even in sickness we are learning something about gratitude, if even in dying we are learning something about ultimate values ... then are not these gifts more worth having than many others that go with security and well-being? What, in the last analysis, do we want to have lived for, and died for?

Finding God in all things means that we can find God even through suffering. "God works with those who love him . . . and turns everything to their good" (Romans 8:28). This does not mean that suffering is good in itself, or that it will inevitably lead us to God. That will depend on what we do with it.

Still less does it mean we should leave other people in their suffering without doing anything to help. Our task is to find God by the way in which we relieve the suffering of others, and by the way we receive our own suffering. While some people become embittered and tedious, we can also often see how others have grown and mellowed even through apparently wasteful, pointless suffering.

We do not have to have a pat answer to why God allows us to suffer in this way now – an easy account of the lesson God intends. Our task is rather, in the dark heart of the mystery of our suffering, to look for a potential way of relating to God.

It may be as simple as praying for help. It is absurd the way we pray so much more when we are in need, and forget to pray in thanksgiving when things are going well, almost as though we were trying to force God to give us a bad time.

Finding God in all things does not take suffering away, but it does help us to find a purpose beyond it and a peace within it.

In ways like this, the First Principle and Foundation asks us to remember what we are here for, and to become aware of what in the end we really want. It does not just tell us that that ought to be God; it invites us to give ourselves the space and time to discover that ultimately it *is* God, that the thirst for God is the deepest of our desires.

But most of the time that awareness simply is not in the foreground, however much we recognize that it should be, and even want it to be. Then it can be fruitful to make a conscious effort to offset our instinctive inclinations by deliberately leaning the other way.

> Thus if our attachment leads us to seek and to hold an office or a benefice, not for the honour and glory of God our Lord, nor for the spiritual welfare of souls, but for our own personal gain and temporal interests, we should strive to rouse a desire for the contrary. (16)

This is called the principle of *agere contra*, which means "to work against", because we work against our inclinations. The point of it is not to make ourselves do everything that we hate, as though the sort of God we worshipped was one who wanted to make us miserable. The point is rather to achieve a better balance, an equilibrium, so that we really are prepared to go in whichever direction God indicates (179).

One Dominican novice-mistress, when asked the purpose of the numerous little disciplines her order demanded, replied that when a sheet of paper had been rolled up tightly for a long time, you could not get it to lie flat without rolling it back in the other direction. Whether or not one would agree with her applications, one can see the point, at least about the roll of paper.

It is similar to the principle that makes some people think that military service had much to be said for it, because the disciplined life of the army gave one a better balance when one came to the more cushy civilian existence afterwards. Or to take a completely contrary example, other people think that if you are likely to end up living a bourgeois little life, with a marriage and a mortgage, then it will do you good to have a more unconventional period before that, wandering the world with a rucksack.

Another way of understanding the *agere contra* is like this. It often happens that we fear something because we have never faced it as a real possibility. Once we imagine the prospect realistically, with a willingness to go that way if need be, then we find our fears are reduced or even vanish entirely. It might be a question of having a baby, or going abroad, or owning up to something wrong we have done.

Once we make ourselves really envisage the prospect we sometimes find that what we were too scared to consider begins to feel right after all. Or we may find that although we are now willing to go that way, it does not feel right, and we can see that with greater clarity than when it was something too awful to face. In this case we do not actually have to *do* the contrary thing; it is enough to take it aboard in imagination to attain a free balance between options.

In ways like this we can recognize the value of leaning in the other direction from our current inclinations, so as to find the point of equilibrium from which an objective decision can be made. This state of mind that is in balance, willing to do whatever is God's will, is called "indifference" or "detachment".

Generosity

One of the biggest struggles of our prayer life is usually over indifference. As we become more interested in religion and devote more time to God in prayer of one form or another, we reach the point at which we feel challenged by the realization that God must not be just one of the priorities, but the over-riding priority of our life.

We hear ourselves praying the "Your will be done" of the Our Father, and we wonder if we mean what we are saying. After all, that was the phrase that Jesus prayed in Gethsemane, as he tried to accept the will of God in his coming passion, and he had enough trouble over saying "yes" to it then. How can we, who are so much weaker and less clear in our minds, manage what Jesus found so difficult?

We can pray "Your will be done" so long as God's will agrees with our own will. But suppose God asked of us something that was hard, something that was even almost impossibly painful? Suppose we were asked to give up our husband or wife? Or we were to be crippled in an accident? Or our children were to die? How could we say "yes" to God's will then?

One Jesuit said that in his struggle over indifference he imagined the loss of his files: looking around his room and wondering what he was attached to they seemed his most precious possession, because all his work depended on them. He prayed, and after quite a tussle found that he would be willing to lose even those if God asked it of him.

But married people and parents have a far more taxing struggle. They know there is nothing in all creation more precious than those they love, their spouse, their children. If they can pray their way through to "Your will be done" about their family, they have really found what indifference can mean.

As Ida Coudenhove said in the last chapter, it is by no means a matter of moderating our love for those dear to us, as though there was such a thing as too great love. Though certainly that mistake has been made again and again in Christian history by generous young women and men who believed that to choose God alone had to mean a celibate life. Rather we can say, our love for our loved ones teaches us what it really can mean to love God, who is always worthy of the greatest love of all.

Offering God our entire will and liberty, out of love, is what Ignatius calls "generosity". The more generously we open ourselves to God in prayer, the more we allow ourselves to be transformed. Even in prayer there are ways of running away from God, by keeping a part of ourselves back in reserve, in case God should ask too much. And so it is good to begin our prayer in an attitude of generosity, with the nearest we can approach to an unconditional self-gift.

Ignatius urges us, in doing the Spiritual Exercises

> to enter upon them with magnanimity and generosity toward our Creator and Lord, and to offer Him our entire will and liberty, that His Divine Majesty may dispose of us and all we possess according to His most holy will. (5)

There are different ways of showing generosity. One is simply an inner disposition of self-giving, a sort of yearning from within. These are the moments when we know the truth of our dependence on God, not just in our heads but deep within our being; we direct ourselves towards the God who alone can satisfy us, but who cannot yet be attained. These are the times when we know we have not yet got what we really want to have, nor yet fully given what we long to give.

Another way is to pray with words of great generosity. We may find that the words stir something within us, to awaken a response that was dormant. But even if we are not much moved in the attempt we will have made an act of will to move in that direction. The few prayers Ignatius gives us are full of generosity. There is the "Lord, teach me to be generous", quoted earlier (see p. 12). Then there is the "Eternal Lord of all things" (quoted on pp. 176), and the "Take and receive" (quoted at the head of Chapter 12).

Another way of showing generosity that goes deeper than warm, generous feelings is in what we call "perseverance" – that decision to stick to a chosen time of prayer even if it is dry, boring or painful, and the regularity in putting aside time for prayer even if we do not feel like it (12). It is like the love we show to our families when we look after them even if we are tired or fed up. Being faithful to someone, whether to a human person or to God, is a real test of love because it shows a choice that goes beyond inclination.

But though generosity can be shown in dry perseverance, it can also be quite a romantic notion, and we can be reminded of Ignatius' drive towards totality in all he did. Once again I quote from Ida Coudenhove, who captures this sense of romance, drawing from the experience of human love to understand the extravagant displays of the saints:

Love is ever travailing for expression. And at the beginning when love is still anxious, still growing, new and strange to itself, it measures itself against other things, tries to fill ever larger vessels, is amazed at itself when it succeeds and demands ever new ways of proving itself to the beloved. It sets itself tests, acts of heroism, displays you might almost call defiant; yes, it is a kind of showing-off before oneself, tests that the beloved by no means demands. Don't you see that in the lives of all the saints? "But God really does not ask this" is the recurrent exclamation of the bourgeois, afraid such exaggeration might be set up as the normal standard. Of course God does not require some of these things. (He requires other things though.) The saint requires it of himself because he is a lover, a young lover who thinks he must continually draw his sweetheart's attention to himself and his love, so that she may have no doubts of it or him; the young and inexperienced lover who is himself not quite sure yet how far his love is equal to his words, how true it rings, and whether, in the excess of his desire it is not greater in intention than in fact. So he tests and proves himself again and again, each time more severely, more madly if you like, and recks nothing of the labour and bitter pains. With every test successfully passed and overcome he exults and leaps, for he can say to himself: "I've achieved that too, for your sake." But when the flood has reached the full, so that all vessels overflow or are swept away, then each is of equal capacity, because they are all equally small, too small. Then to be together in silence means as much as or more than the most exuberant declaration or gesture, and hardly noticeable service equals the most splendid gift. Doesn't this help us to understand why believers under the Old Covenant or pious heathens could slaughter fifty thousand beasts to do homage to God – only to attain the painful realization that the most gorgeous hecatomb could not fill the gulf between man and Deity? The Christian on the other hand takes a little wafer and some drops of wine and water, prays: *suscipe sancte Pater* ["receive, holy Father" – words from the Latin mass], and knows himself accepted in this sign, which is indeed only a sign, so accepted that the miracle which he craves for himself, to be changed into the living Christ, takes place representatively in the sign; he knows that his sign has been so fully accepted – that God replies to it by *His* gift, His Son.

(*Essays in Order*, pp. 73–4)

This is the right context to understand mortification, self-denial and penance (of which more will be said in Chapter 8)

– not as something gloomy and negative, but as the free flowing of our love for God. I end this chapter with some words from Mother Julian of Norwich, who, while speaking of giving up everything for God, can still convey a sense of joy about it.

No soul can have rest until it finds created things are empty. When the soul gives up all for love, so that it can have him that is all, then it finds true rest.

For he is endless and has made us for his own self only, and has restored us by his blessed Passion, and keeps us in his blessed love. And he does all this through his goodness.

God of your goodness give me yourself, for you are enough for me and I may ask nothing that is less, that may be full worship to you. And if I ask anything that is less, I am always wanting – but only in you I have all.

(*Showings*, Chapter 5)

3

Learning to Pray

It is not much knowledge that fills and satisfies the soul, but the intimate understanding and relish of the truth. (2)

Prayer is rather like chewing the cud: you take a little and you stay with it until you have drained out all the goodness – not all the goodness that will ever be got out, but all that is there for you for the time being. You relish the word of God, until it becomes intimate to you, and fills your consciousness.

A little Latin phrase that captures this simple lesson is this: *non multa, sed multum*, which can be clumsily translated "not many things, but much". We may remember that Jesus said something very similar: "In praying do not heap up empty phrases as the Gentiles do; for they think that they will be heard for their many words." (Matthew 6:7)

This means that prayer is a slow activity, but a satisfying one. For this reason if for no other we find prayer rather hard work, because we are used to whizzing around in a twentieth-century world where life is generally fast and unsatisfying.

When we pray the first thing we do is to change gear dramatically, to, as it were, get out of the fast car tearing down the motorway and into a little donkey cart ambling gently among the fields and hills. It is the change that is irksome. We want to say to our prayer, "Get on with it. This is boring. What's next?" We have really to make ourselves relax and grow accustomed to the new rhythm. Then it ceases to be frustrating and we begin to find it is the best time of the day.

"It is not much knowledge that fills and satisfies the soul, but the intimate understanding and relish of the truth." For academically-minded people this is something that may be quite difficult at first, conditioned as they are to consume book after book, always trying to step up their reading speed. When they find that they are urged, not to read sixty pages in an hour, but in the same time to get through perhaps five verses of one chapter of the Bible, they are either horrified or profoundly relieved.

And when they then find that their accustomed habits of critical analysis of reading matter are not exactly what is called for, they may feel at a loss again. It is not that keen, critical thought is of no use in prayer, but it is only a tool; in itself it does not constitute prayer.

Something else has to happen before prayer begins, something along the lines of bowing down in the presence of God and listening to what this means for me. Some people hate considering what "this means for me", so they run away from it into lofty, rational thought that need not touch them, just as the pre-adolescent child will run away from being kissed.

We do not have to have a complicated theory of prayer to grasp this point for it is quite apparent and obvious: there is a difference between sitting at my desk to study a text, and putting myself in the presence of God to pray about it (whether sitting at my desk or not, preferably not). People generally know what prayer is without elaborate definitions, even small children know, because prayer is a natural activity, a natural instinct.

One outcome of this is that when we listen to the fruits of other people's prayer, this is not the sort of matter to which we take a searchlight to show how thoroughly illogical or unorthodox it is. We are dealing with something that is touched by the Spirit, that belongs to the precious inter-relationship of a person with their God, and that the rude outsider ought to show a certain reverence for, even if the terms in which it is expressed sound alien or unfortunate.

Ignatius calls this the Presupposition: in the context of spiritual direction he says

> it is necessary to suppose that every good Christian is more ready to put a good interpretation on another's statement than to condemn it as false. If an orthodox construction cannot be put on a proposition, the one who made it should be asked how they understand it. If they are in error, they should be corrected with all kindness. If this does not suffice, all appropriate means should be used to bring them to a correct interpretation, and so defend the proposition from error. (22)

There are suitable contexts for hatchet-jobs on theological utterances, but listening to other people's prayer experiences is not one of them. What someone is brave enough to share with us – whether in a prayer group, or individual direction, or a letter, or a book even – we should receive with appreciation and respect.

There is another way in which we can show reverence for the work of the Holy Spirit in other people's prayer. It is one which ordained ministers can find very difficult because they are so used to being treated as experts. It is basically to shut up and get out of the way. The temptation is to say too much, to explain too fully, to do too much of the work themselves, instead of trusting that the Holy Spirit can perfectly well work in another person without their intervention.

"Adhere to the points, and add only a short or summary explanation", says Ignatius (2). This is because we experience "greater spiritual relish and fruit" (2) if we have our own insight into a text than if someone else had made the same points to us. But it often happens that a priest or preacher, especially for example in a retreat, will spend so long telling us the meaning of a scripture passage, that if we are supposed to

51

pray on it afterwards we either have to spend our time admiring the wisdom of his words, or deliberately forgetting about them so that we can get on with a different line of our own. One Anglican ordinand said that when his college held retreats he used to need half an hour to recover from each address before he could get on with the business of making his retreat, and he said it quite simply and unpretentiously.

Preaching on scripture is a precious and beautiful task, but it is not a good preparation for someone else's prayer unless it is kept brief. Similarly, urging someone to take some course of action may be quite appropriate in many circumstances, but if it is preparatory to them praying over the same question it can impede the equilibrium of which we spoke in the last chapter, so that they have difficulty listening to the promptings of the Spirit. In short, it is difficult for them to know if they are being influenced by God or by the person who last spoke to them.

These two rules – be brief in your presentation of scripture, and avoid telling other people what to do with their lives – apply with very special rigour if you are directing someone in retreat, because of the increased vulnerability of retreatants, as they open themselves in an intense and prolonged way to encounter with God. But to a lesser extent we can see the wisdom of these recommendations at other levels and in other situations.

The more the so-called experts in the Church behave, and are treated, as though they are the only ones who can interpret scripture, the less do the so-called non-experts feel the confidence that they too can listen to the Word of God in prayer. They are given the impression that their thoughts are second-best, so they feel discouraged in their meditation before they start.

If the Church is to encourage ordinary people to pray, it has to begin by helping them believe that even they can do it, or rather that the Holy Spirit can do it even in them. And that means giving them sufficient help and encouragement, but not more than sufficient so as to take away from their own contribution.

If you are in the position of helping others learn to pray, your task is essentially one of "facilitation" (as it is called in the contemporary jargon of spirituality). In other words you slip into the background as much as possible, because your work is to get things out of other people, not to do the work yourself.

It is like helping someone learn to ride a bicycle, or learn to swim; you keep your touch as light as possible on the back of the saddle, or under their tummy. If you gave them too much support it would not be surprising if they fell off, or sank, as soon as you let go.

Here is what Ignatius said to encourage those giving the Spiritual Exercises to trust that God would work in prayer if only they kept out of the way. Bearing in mind particularly the times of decision-making, Ignatius comments:

While one is engaged in the Spiritual Exercises, it is more suitable and much better that the Creator and Lord in person communicate himself to the devout soul in quest of the divine will, that he inflame it with his love and praise, and dispose it for the way in which it could better serve God in the future. Therefore, the director of the Exercises, as a balance at equilibrium, without leaning to one side or the other, should permit the Creator to deal directly with the creature, and the creature directly with its Creator and Lord. (15)

There is a corresponding moral if we are learning to pray rather than helping others learn: we will not get far if we are too dependent on our book or our priest or our prayer group. If, as soon as a prop of that sort is removed, we lose our inspiration, then we need to remember Ignatius' words about God inflaming us with love and praise as he communicates with us in person, not via intermediaries. God should be allowed to deal with us directly, and we should allow ourselves to deal with God directly.

Unless we are prepared to try to pray on our own there is not any point in looking for assistance. We suffer from the temptation to read one book on prayer after another, hoping that sometime the miracle will occur when we suddenly find instant contemplation overwhelming us without any of the preparatory discipline.

Perhaps the best analogy, rather than bicycling or swimming, is learning a language: prayer is the language with which we speak to God. Many people excuse their inability to talk foreign languages by pretending they do not have a natural flair for languages, as though it was a rather rare gift to be able to talk anything other than English. It is the same with prayer: people tend to imagine that you need some special contemplative vocation before it will be worthwhile spending even brief periods of time in prayer.

However I have often observed how the most important factor in learning a foreign language is not natural flair but simple motivation. People who are motivated learn quickly and without fuss, whether they are spurred on by being in love with a foreigner, or just by living in a society where it is taken for granted that you can do it (as the Africans and the Poles and the Dutch show us, as they speak three, four or five languages fluently).

But in any case, learning to pray is not like learning to speak a foreign language, as much as like learning to speak the mother-tongue. Because we all can do this we tend to forget, until we come in touch with young children, that we are not born speaking English, but take a few years to learn. And yet what we learn to do is something that comes completely naturally. Language is an intrinsic talent that will produce symptoms of frustration if it is not developed.

It is the same with prayer. Everyone needs to pray, and everyone can pray, whether they are young or old or stupid or clever. But we may pray more expressively and less laboriously if we have learned something of the potentialities of the language from others, and if we have become familiar with its use through speaking it.

It is not just a matter of learning to say what we want to say anyway, but, as with language, developing a sensitivity and responsiveness that is authentic within us but undeveloped. Praying, like talking, is not just an expression of what we already know, but is a creative and transforming process.

Choosing a time

After so many exhortations to put theory into practice, it is time to give some more concrete advice on what we can do in prayer. The next chapter will go through a prayer period, step by step, but in this chapter we will look at a few important preliminary choices.

Preliminaries are important, not because they make the exercise more long-winded and complicated and therefore virtuous, as the over-scrupulous part of our conscience may be whispering, but on the contrary, because they make the exercise easier. If we just stumble in we may find that we have chosen a bad time, a bad place and a bad method. And if that is the case we are not likely to look forward to it next time, if there is a next time.

Time is the first question to consider. What can we do to choose a good time? In the first place we need to distinguish the prayer that we make as we do other things – as we travel in the car, for example, or as we lie in the bath – from prayer that we make when we are doing nothing else, the prayer that we make when we are not killing two birds with one stone, but when we have set aside a time for God alone. Both sorts of prayer are good, both are beautiful, but it is the latter sort that I shall principally be talking about, because it is the latter sort that provides the easier conditions for prayer. It is not surprising if we get distracted if we are trying to drive a car at the same time.

So the first decision is "Am I going to pray at a time when I can devote my entire being to doing nothing else?" If we assume a positive answer to that, the next question is "OK, when on earth am I going to have time to do that?" We will find we have time if praying is currently sufficiently high up on our list of priorities. Let us suppose that it is, and that we are determined to make a time somehow.

One way in which people make time is by getting up earlier in the morning. Some people find this good: their minds are clear, the lines to God are open, the world is peacefully poised to bring forth the new day's life, and their own individual day is consecrated with a prayer that embraces all they do until nightfall. It is a time when one can truly say, with Hopkins:

And for all this, nature is never spent;
  There lives the dearest freshness deep down things;
And though the last lights off the black West went
  Oh, morning, at the brown brink eastward, springs –
Because the Holy Ghost over the bent
  World broods with warm breast and with ah! bright wings.
                                        (*God's Grandeur*)

On the other hand, some other people can imagine few greater forms of daily torture than having to wrench themselves out of their warm beds to embark on the ill-fated attempt to meditate before they have even woken up properly. They, perhaps, might be happier praying at night-time – which is also a time of stillness in the world, when the presence of God may be sensed through the silence. In a family home one really does need to get rid of the other people by one means or another before one can fully relax and open before God. If they are asleep it is ideal. Every parent knows the great burden that is lifted off their shoulders once the children have gone to bed.

But others are just too tired at night-time. For them it would be giving the fag-end of the day to God, and they would be painfully trying to keep their eyelids from drooping when all they want to do is go to sleep.

It may be possible for a while when children are very young to pray in the early evening – if, for example, they go to bed at 6.00 and the evening meal is not till after 7.00. Or if there is a toddler who has a day-time snooze it may be possible to have a half-hour in the afternoon. But any plan like this is subject to rearrangement as children grow older and their timetable alters.

People without children but with full-time jobs do not necessarily have it easier. People with both children and full-time jobs have it hardest of all.

An idea that worked for one man was to put a "Do not disturb" notice on his office door during lunch hour. A woman who had a heavy teaching load, a long journey, and an evening full of preparation for the next day's classes, found that the only time she could manage was as soon as she got home from work, when she was absolutely exhausted; and yet she found that however bad the time it was so much better than having no time at all that it was worth keeping the prayer going. There are few of us, after all, who do not have at least five or ten minutes in the day flopped in a chair or in front of the television or having a drink in the pub. And why not, instead of just flopping, do something enriching and rejuvenating at the same time?

After all, if there is something we want to do we can find time for it somehow, whether it is caring for a new baby or learning how to work a new computer or looking around for a new house. It is all a question of priorities.

Now let us suppose that we have found a time, at least

provisionally. We will make things easier for ourselves if, as far as possible, we make that a regular time. Of course we should be ready to alter if it is not working out well, or if we can find a better time, or if our timetable changes. But if we can set up a regular daily rhythm then we relieve ourselves of the burden of deciding anew each day when to fit our prayer in, and we may find ourselves actually feeling like praying when we reach that hour. It is like the way we may feel like a cup of coffee at 11.00, or a cup of tea at 4.00, or a glass of sherry at 7.00, or a pint of beer at 9.00, because that is what we have become used to. Human beings are creatures of habit, and we must remember the rule "use what helps".

We may also find, if we have a regular rhythm, that during the rest of the day we feel happy to look back to the last prayer time, or to look forward to the next one. This is a good sense, and one worth developing, because that pleasant thought within us is itself a prayer, a way of saying "I want to be with you, God". Ignatius suggested in particular that we should let our thoughts turn this way at the last moment of the day, in bed, before we fall asleep, especially if praying is the first thing we plan to do in the morning (73).

Some people work differently. If you really can wait until the moment in the day when you feel sufficiently poised and peaceful to want to turn to prayer, not knowing when that will be from one day till the next, then you are lucky. It is beautiful to do it that way. But realize that few people can cope with that degree of unpredictability, and maintain an active prayer life over a period of time.

The question now is not just "When?" but "How long?"

The traditional Ignatian prayer time is one hour. That may sound horrifying, and it would usually be a mistake for someone unused to set-aside times of prayer to begin with such a marathon: they might spend fifty-nine minutes longing for it to come to an end. But we should not just assume that

that will always be beyond our abilities. The taste for prayer can grow, from small beginnings, far beyond our expectations.

After a little practice we will find that when we have a long period like that we lose much of the tension and anxiety about how to fill the time. We find we can stretch and unfold before God without worrying unduly if there is a seemingly fruitless patch: there is enough time for a lot to happen in an hour, and for us to pass through several phases. It often happens that we go through a bad stage somewhere in the middle, when we are looking at our watch again and again, and then the last ten minutes turn out to be the best of all, perhaps because God wants to reward us at that time, perhaps because as we near the end we lose some of our tension about perseverance.

Particularly in time of retreat there is great value in accustoming ourselves to long sessions like a half-hour or an hour, and in closed retreat the discipline is incomparably easier because the other pressures are lifted and we move into a new rhythm. But in ordinary life we must be more gentle with ourselves. For some people ten minutes is a good time to choose. For others, twenty. For others, forty.

But what may be best is not to decide on any period of time in advance, but to pray for as long as our prayer takes. We stop when we want – not at the first moment we feel bored, but when we feel sufficiently satisfied to not mind bringing the session to a close. It might be three minutes, it might be thirty, but whichever it is is worth noticing from our watch, simply from the point of view of self-awareness. We may surprise ourselves.

Choosing a place

So much for time. Place is also an important preliminary, because we can be affected very much by where we are, and we want to use what helps and avoid what hinders.

If we ask ourselves what places we have been in that we have found prayerful, that have actually drawn us into prayer by their holiness, the answer may be a church or it may be a natural beauty spot. Old churches, churches that house the tomb of a saint, churches that are filled with lighted candles as the token of others' prayers – these can have an extraordinary power over awakening our thirst for God.

Or a view from the top of a mountain can do the same, or a moonlit sea, or a garden full of fragrant flowers. In *Sadhana* (the book I have already mentioned on p. 24) Anthony de Mello points out how important the choice of place was for Jesus:

> Has it ever occurred to you that Jesus, that master in the art of prayer, would take the trouble to walk up a hill in order to pray? Like all great contemplatives he was aware that the place in which we pray has an influence on the quality of our prayer. (p. 62)

We might wish that we could bring one of these scenes home with us, to enter into it whenever we wished to find God in prayer. In a sense we can, by using our imagination, and we look at that in the section on "composition of place" in the next chapter. But for now we are considering what we can do physically, rather than imaginatively, to find a place that helps us pray.

One possibility is actually to go to a place that helps us pray. Once in a while it can be a splendid idea to go, as Jesus did, up a hill or mountain. But I assume we will not be able to do that very often. Some people, especially those who live in lovely countryside, may choose to pray outside. One woman I knew used to include a walk across a meadow in her prayer, and found her prayer much less rich when she omitted it. Sheila Cassidy, in her book *Prayer for Pilgrims*, talks of praying as she sits "huddled in the cold on a muddy river bank at half past six on an October morning"; it may not sound very inviting, and yet "there are the days when the early morning is filled with magic and the swirling mist over the valley is the pillar of cloud that barely conceals the unknowable, untouchable, the Alpha of my being." (pp. 74, 76) If going out helps, go out. For myself I have only found praying outside helpful in an Italian summer. It is principally a matter of being cold.

There are places we can go to which are indoors, most obviously churches. One man doing the Spiritual Exercises in a 19th annotation retreat worked out a daily rhythm of slipping into his church on the way home. His place of prayer was always ready and waiting for him, and no household hassles of screaming kids or telephones could come between him and the God he was seeking. There is something secret and rather fun about having a whole church all to ourselves. Or, if there are other people praying there, there is a communion of prayer that is precious in another way. For some Catholics, the presence of the Blessed Sacrament is the greatest aid to prayer that can be, for our God is there, truly present in the tabernacle, and the red glow of the sanctuary lamp reflects the warmth that we feel in our hearts.

If we pray in our own home (and that is what most people choose) then it is an enormous help if we can, in one way or another, make a special prayer place. One of the simplest ways of transforming a perfectly ordinary room into a place of prayer is by the small symbol of a lighted candle: we light it when we pray and blow it out when we finish. We do not have it alight at other times, so the candle always reminds us of the presence of God, and as it burns it gives us support by, as it were, praying with us. What is more, if it is dark when we light it the room will look quite different, and the concentration of all light in that one spot will mirror the concentration of our mind and heart on God.

Another simple way of marking a place of prayer in an ordinary room is by having a small shelf or corner, where we place something that speaks to us of God. It may be a religious postcard; it may be a crucifix; it may be a poster; it may be a shell, or a flower in a vase. We may use one object, or we may make a little shrine with a number of things. One woman used to have a postcard of the raising of Lazarus on her mantlepiece, and hidden behind it a photo of her baby who had died.

If we want something more private, we can create a prayer space that can be dismantled again afterwards. For example, we can sit with our Bible open before us and take out from its pages a picture that is special to us. That immediately creates a prayerful environment. Or we can sit in a chair that we do not usually sit in, or turn it to face a direction it does not usually face; or we can sit cross-legged on a particular spot on the carpet used only for prayer; or we can sit on a large cushion that no one will know is for us a prayer cushion; or kneel on one of the little wooden prayer stools with a sloping top that have become popular and that can tuck away under the bed; or we can have a rug that we unroll just for prayer – a prayer mat. We do not have to do any of these things, of course. There is no point unless they are helpful.

What may be most helpful of all is to have a room just for prayer. That may sound rather ambitious, but my own little prayer-hole is a cupboard under the stairs too low even to stand up in: if it was not used for prayer it would be full of boxes; well, half of it is – I have the other half. I put there the religious pictures and objects that mean most to me, and I think if I did not have it I would find regular prayer very difficult indeed. Someone else uses the triangular space made by a dormer window in a converted attic: with her back to the rest of the attic it feels like a little room of its own. Someone else again has a garden hut, and another person a converted pigsty. Another couple, who have eight children and not a particularly large house, put aside an entire bedroom as a prayer room. And yet another couple have a large tower room at the top of the house, almost a chapel, though they call it the prayer room. One begins to feel less embarrassed about wanting a place set aside for prayer when one knows that there are others who do the same.

The places I have mentioned belong to laity, but more and more religious houses too are setting aside a room to be an oratory; I am not talking of a specially built chapel, but just an ordinary room, with a soft carpet and some cushions, and maybe a simple tabernacle or maybe not. Many religious find that more homely and intimate to pray in than the more forbidding chapel.

One great advantage of praying at home is that it is more private, so that we will be less inhibited if we feel drawn to pray out loud (in tongues, or not) or to lie down on our faces before the holiness of God, or to raise our hands to heaven, or to weep (88). We may feel more alone with God in the privacy of our home, than in a field or a church. "When you pray, go into your room and shut the door and pray to your Father who is in secret; and your Father who sees in secret will reward you." (Matthew 6:6)

4

Structuring a Prayer Time

Second Week. First Day and First contemplation.
*This is a contemplation on the incarnation. After the preparatory
prayer and three preludes there are three points and a colloquy.
(101)*

"This", you may say, "is just the sort of thing that puts me off.
Whoever wants to pray in terms of a preparatory prayer, three
preludes, three points and a colloquy, as though they were
laying out an account sheet in columns? This is death to the
deep mystery of prayer. And what on earth are these absurd
terms supposed to mean anyway?"

That is a healthy reaction, though it can sometimes have a
touch of snobbery in it, as though anyone who could not
effortlessly slip into the same dark depths of God that I can is
not praying properly at all.

But there is nothing to fear. A structure of this kind is never
more than provisional. If your prayer has lifted you into a
communion with God from which you do not want to move,
then you should stay there. To try to get on with the next
point that you have been set would be to refuse the gift God is
offering at that moment, and to work according to the dictates
of human beings rather than the inspiration of the Spirit. It is
always a firm Ignatian rule to stay where you are as long as you
find there what you are seeking "without any eagerness to go
on till I have been satisfied" (76).

All this business of preludes and points and so on, is
essentially a way Ignatius has of getting us to notice some of
the diverse kinds of things that we do anyway when we pray.

Using the language analogy again, it is like studying grammar. We will not get on very well with grammar if we do not have a natural sense of language – we will find it hard to recognize an adverbial phrase or whatever – and similarly we will not have much idea of what Ignatius means by his terms if we do not have experiences of prayer to which they correspond. We use language before we learn grammar, and we begin to pray before we are told about preludes and colloquies.

Anyone who tries to use language fluently and expressively will be well advised to have at least a basic knowledge of grammar, so that they can isolate the elements of speech and notice how they operate; so too anyone who wishes to grow in prayer will be much helped if they have some idea of the different elements that can be used in prayer and the way they can lead into each other. To look at some of the things we do when we pray need not come between us and God any more than learning grammar need stop us writing poetry. It will only get in the way if we keep it in the forefront, as though we could not write a line or send a yearning heavenwards without running through in our mind "Now what comes next? Subject . . . verb . . . object / Preparatory prayer . . . preludes . . . points". These are processes that should come instinctively, even if we have never heard of a verb or a prelude.

This chapter may seem to do rather a lot of complicated dissection, but the structure suggested is to be followed in prayer only (yet again) in so far as it helps. If we can recognize something of the same elements in our prayer, but they come in a different order, that is nothing to worry about: Ignatius gives us a classic pattern, but there will always be variations.

In any case, the next chapter – "Reading, Meditating, Praying" – will cover the same ground again but with a much simpler scheme, so there is no need to feel you have to remember and follow everything in this chapter. With all those qualifications, let us now go through a prayer period, step by step.

Preparation

In order to enter our prayer wholeheartedly and reverently it can be valuable to have a few moments' preparation. We want to avoid frittering away our prayer time over questions like "What shall I pray on? Shall I use scripture? Let me look through the Bible and find a passage that I like."

And so, at the very least we must make sure that we have what we need ready to hand. If we are going to light a candle we will make sure we have matches. If we are going to use a set prayer that we do not know by heart, we will find a copy. If we are going to look at a picture we will choose the one we want. If we are going to use our Bible we will have to fetch it. If we are going to pray on the Good Samaritan we will have to find the place.

Ignatius warns that the consideration of one mystery can interfere with the contemplation of another (127), which is a way of reminding us of the concentration and focusing that is needed in prayer. If we can settle on what it is that we wish to pray over even before we enter our prayer, setting aside not just the bustle of our lives but also the tempting distractions of other good and religious thoughts, then we are making the kind of preparation that disposes us for good prayer.

We cannot pray about everything all at once, no matter how Christian it is, so we will have to make a conscientious choice, and then follow it through. We may take our prompting from some external source, like the liturgical year or the plan of a retreat; we may take it from a pattern we have chosen for ourselves, like a systematic meditation on John's gospel; or we may take it from the needs of our life at the time, like choosing the death of John the Baptist, for example, when we have heard of the death of one of our relatives or friends.

For the same reason it may be better to read once through the scripture passage we have chosen before we begin to pray, so that we have an overview in our head from which to pause and examine details more closely. It is good to avoid reading at length during times of prayer; if we read it should be a little, so that we can dwell on it, intimately understanding it and relishing it, as Ignatius said (see p. 49). So it is often worthwhile to do a little preparatory reading before we begin.

With many stories we will have a choice of gospels anyway, and it will be good to have found the account we want to use, or to have them all at the back of our mind so that we can bring elements of Matthew's version into the Lucan text before us, for example. We may find that once we have begun to pray we do not want to open our eyes to look at the passage again, and if we have done our preparation we will not need to.

How much we should stick to our planned subject matter depends on the situation. In times of retreat it is important not to chop and change – we plan a day at a time and we stay within that plan, at least to the extent of staying with the same mystery though it may take unsuspected turnings. Because a retreat is an especially intense time of prayer it may be that where we feel reluctance or difficulty we are facing a block that needs to be worked through.

But out of retreat we need not discipline ourselves so exactly. If when we place ourselves in the presence of God we feel drawn by a different mystery or by a different type of prayer altogether it may be right to follow it. In or out of retreat it is reasonable to say that it is good to use enough planning to help us enter the prayer wholeheartedly and without delay, but not so much as to tell God what we think ought to happen.

The preparation is not just a matter of practicalities, but an inner turning towards God. Just as we may have looked forward to our prayer time from another point in the day (see p. 58), so we look forward to it now as something that is just about to begin.

As soon as I recall that it is time for the exercise in which I ought to engage, before proceeding to it, I will call to mind, where I am going, before whom I am to appear, and briefly sum up the exercise. (131)

In any case we should not fuss or delay over this preparation, which Ignatius says should be brief. Our eyes should not be on making a good preparation but on making a good prayer: that is what we want to get on with.

Preparatory prayer

As we enter our prayer we can remember Ignatius' suggestion (see p. 26) that we can make even walking into the place where we are going to meditate an act of prayer in itself. We settle into the position for prayer that suits us (see pp. 23–7). Then, with what is (if we think about it) an act of will or choice (see p. 28), we make the preparatory prayer. The preparatory prayer is to be distinguished from the preparation for prayer: the latter is what we do before we have begun to pray, the former is the first thing we do when we pray.

The preparatory prayer, as explained above (see p. 19), recalls the First Principle and Foundation. It is the act of directing myself towards God, placing myself in the presence of God and asking for help, reaffirming my commitment to make my whole life centre on God. This, in one way or another, is what everyone does when they begin to pray, whether or not they call it the preparatory prayer. They do not have to use Ignatius' formula of begging for grace that everything I intend and do may be for the praise and service of God, because there are so many ways of expressing the same desire, most of them non-verbal. As often as not it is just a swing of the heart. But it could equally well be the picking up of a crucifix to gaze at.

Prayer begins when we become still and know, in that stillness, that God is there, and when we choose to be there, challenged by the divine presence. There may be a strong sense of presence, so that we do not want to do or say anything else for a long time. Or it may be a dry choice with no sensible reward. That is of no less value in God's eyes. As long as we have done what is reasonable to dispose ourselves, it is up to God whether we feel anything very much. What matters is that we choose to be there. "Lord, it is good for us to be here." (Matthew 17:4)

The First Prelude: the history

When we are ready – it may be a minute or a half-hour – we can begin to turn to our chosen subject matter. If we are praying on a story from scripture, we will recall it to our mind, or re-read it. This First Prelude is what Ignatius calls "the history of the mystery" (111). We have not yet begun a deep and slow attention to detail, though that will soon begin to develop.

If our prayer is not going to be based on an event from the Bible, then this prelude does not apply, because there is no clear history to recall. In that case there are two preludes instead of three. I find it simpler to think in terms of omitting the First Prelude, rather than renumbering the Second and Third Preludes as the First and Second.

The word "mystery" may puzzle some people. If for "mystery" you read "event" or "story" you will not go far wrong. The word "mystery" captures the sense that the events of salvation history do not yield all their truth at the first reading, but contain secret depths.

Catholics often use the word "mystery" without worrying about what it means, because the rosary has five joyful mysteries, five sorrowful mysteries, and five glorious mysteries; none of these refer to abstract ideas but to historical events like the annunciation and the nativity, in which a wider truth is contained.

Christianity is not just a philosophy: it tells us what actually happened, what God did in the history of the world. That is why the word "mystery", for Christians, does not mean an abstract truth but something that happened.

As we recall the history of the mystery, we will find that images begin to form in our mind, and these are to be welcomed. Some of Ignatius' examples have a certain charm. He sees the Three Divine Persons looking down at the circuit of the earth and seeing what a mess we are making of our lives (102). He sees Mary about nine months pregnant, sitting on an ass and accompanied not only by Joseph but also by a maidservant leading an ox (111). As these images begin to form, we are naturally moving into the Second Prelude, which is explicitly the work of the imagination.

The Second Prelude: composition of place

Ignatius calls the Second Prelude "a composition, seeing the place" (103). This is usually abbreviated to "a composition of place", but Anthony de Mello (*Sadhana*, p. 63) prefers the longer phrase because it carries an implication that we are not just composing a picture but, as we contemplate our mental image, allowing ourselves to become composed – a good word for the concentrated, relaxed, quiet state of mind that disposes us for prayer.

We are beginning to touch here on the whole area of imaginative prayer, and the next chapter will explore this further. The Second Prelude is a little imaginative input that comes early in our prayer, even if the rest of our prayer is not going to be primarily imaginative in form.

The "composition of place" is one of the Ignatian terms

that have become quite well-known even among people who do not know what it means. It refers to something very simple: we look at the place where the scene is happening. If we are praying, for example, on the journey of the pregnant Mary to Bethlehem, then we see in imagination the road: "Consider its length, its breadth; whether level, or through valleys and over hills" (112).

Now Ignatius, whose pilgrimage to the Holy Land had been an important event soon after his conversion, does not tell us what that road – which he had presumably seen – was actually like. That is not the point. The point is to have your own picture, the image that arises in your imagination when you have put yourself in the hands of the Holy Spirit in prayer. That will be the picture that belongs to your relationship to God as you pray over this mystery. It could be a busy motorway or it could be a starlit footpath: either could be the setting in which God chooses to communicate to you.

It is rather like the way we may look at different paintings of, say, the Last Supper. Each one helps the mystery to become more vivid to us, and there is no contradiction if in one the table is round, in another rectangular, if in one Jesus is wearing a white robe, in another coloured garments, if in one the room is grand and full of servants, in another plain and empty apart from the apostles. What the particularities are does not matter, but what matters is that there should be particularities, because they help the scene to become real and vivid and memorable. What we are touched by, through the medium of the physical details, is a spiritual truth. The same applies if the painting is of the nativity, or the crucifixion, or any other mystery.

Every time we make the Second Prelude Ignatius asks us the same basic and seemingly dull questions about how we see the place. We are to consider "the garden [of Gethsemane], its breadth, its length, and appearance" (202). We are "to consider the way from Bethany to Jerusalem,

71

whether narrow or broad, whether level, etc.; also the place of the Supper, whether great or small, whether of this or that appearance" (192). For the appearance after the resurrection to Mary his mother "it will be to see the arrangement of the holy sepulchre and the place or house of our Lady. I will note its different parts, and also her room, her oratory, etc." (220). Note Ignatius' delightful image of Mary having a private oratory among the rooms of her house.

We may have noticed that some of the scenes Ignatius suggests are not explicitly mentioned in the scriptures but are inferred to have happened. The gospels give no details of Mary's journey to Bethlehem, nor of Jesus' journey from Bethany to Jerusalem, yet since these people went to those places there must have been a journey, and Ignatius considers it worthwhile journeying with them. Nor do we have an account of the circumstances in which the risen Jesus was first seen by his mother, but that does not stop Ignatius basing a meditation on the imagined event.

We can use this Prelude whether our prayer time is to be devoted to a mystery of scripture or not, but if not then it needs a broader understanding.

When the contemplation or meditation is on something visible, for example, when we contemplate Christ our Lord, the representation will consist in seeing in imagination the material place where the object is that we wish to contemplate. I said the material place, for example, the temple, or the mountain where Jesus or his Mother is, according to the subject matter of the contemplation.

In a case where the subject matter is not visible, as here in a meditation on sin, the representation will be to see in imagination my soul as a prisoner in this corruptible body, and to consider my whole composite being as an exile here on earth, cast out to live among brute beasts. (47)

Or, for example, when the subject matter is the call Christ makes to us, we are invited to make a composition of place by seeing "in imagination the synagogues, villages, and towns where Christ our Lord preached" (91). Or, when the subject matter is to contemplate the love of God, the composition of place is "to behold myself standing in the presence of God our Lord and of his angels and saints, who intercede for me" (232).

This may at first sound rather strange and puzzling, but the basic principle behind it becomes quite compelling once it is grasped. There are many ways in which people have learnt to focus their concentration for prayer. They may say a mantra over and over, or gaze at a mandala (a symbolic design). If they are more traditional in their devotions they may say a litany or gaze at the tabernacle.

We have already looked at some of the awareness exercises that can be used to compose ourselves in a state of still concentration (see pp. 24–5). Then, towards the end of the last chapter, we considered how a lighted candle, or a picture, or a flower in a vase can be a helpful visual focus. The composition of place is the imaginative equivalent to all these disciplines of concentration.

Instead of looking at a real dried leaf or skyscape tinged with pink we can look at one in our imagination, and in many ways that is better because it will be an image that springs out of our prayer and therefore fits where we are with God.

An image I sometimes use for composition of place is to see a pool with ripples all over its surface; then, as I watch and become quieter and more composed, I see the ripples fade, until the water is clear and I can gaze down through the water and see what lies at the bottom of the pool. When I reach this point I am ready to move beyond the Prelude, into the matter of the prayer.

When we look more fully at imaginative contemplation in

the next chapter we will be following whole scenes. The Second Prelude does not go this far. We set the scene. We see the place. We have a visual context for our prayer. That is enough for the time being.

The Third Prelude: what I want

"I will ask God our Lord for what I want and desire", says Ignatius (48, see also 55, 104, 193, 203, 221, 233). "What I want" – in Latin *id quod volo* – is of supreme importance in prayer, and Ignatius draws our attention to it with regular insistence. Every meditation includes prayer for what it is that I want.

At first this could sound rather childish, as though we were being brought back from our high-minded, scriptural ideas to a list of wants like "Please may it not rain on our weekend trip, and please may we get the new pay deal we are striking for . . ." But it is not that.

Ignatius says:

> The petition made in this prelude must be according to the subject matter. Thus in a contemplation on the Resurrection I will ask for joy with Christ in joy. In one on the passion, I will ask for sorrow, tears, and anguish with Christ in anguish (48).

The regular petition (petition means an asking prayer) that we make for most mysteries in the life of Christ is

> an intimate knowledge of our Lord, who has become human for me, that I may love him more and follow him more closely. (104)

One of the important things about this petition for what I want is the recognition that all is grace. No matter how many hours I spend in prayer, I cannot achieve what I want by my own efforts. I can only ask. I dispose myself, and I ask for the grace. The rest is up to God. Sometimes the Third Prelude is called the prayer for particular grace (as opposed to the general grace asked for in the preparatory prayer).

One may be tempted to protest, "But that high-sounding petition is not 'what I want'. My wants are not nearly as exalted as that. Ignatius seems to be telling us to put on a false face, and to try to screw ourselves up to pious emotions that we do not have."

This objection is valuable, because in sorting it out we begin to understand something profound about what prayer is about. "What I want and desire" is somewhere between the petitions for my consciously felt, minor, earthly wants, and the higher desires that are not yet mine. Prayer happens in the tension between the two. Let me explain what I mean by a story from John's gospel:

> The next day again John was standing with two of his disciples; and he looked at Jesus as he walked, and said, "Behold, the Lamb of God!" The two disciples heard him say this, and they followed Jesus. Jesus turned, and saw them following, and said to them, "What do you seek?" And they said to him, "Rabbi" (which means Teacher) "where are you staying?" He said to them, "Come and see." They came and saw where he was staying; and they stayed with him that day. (John 1:35–9)

When Jesus asked them what they were seeking, they did not really know. So they answered with other questions, a request to see where Jesus lived. In going to see where he lived, and in staying all day with him, they were beginning to answer, for themselves and for Jesus, the question about what they were looking for. They were seeking to know Jesus better, with the knowledge from which love springs, and from that love, discipleship. What they really wanted, though as yet they hardly knew it, was "an intimate knowledge of our Lord, who has become human for me, that I may love him more and follow him more closely."

We make the Third Prelude at the point of our prayer when we have begun to follow Jesus, but not yet gone very far. Think of it like this: when we are beginning to settle into our prayer we let the Lord turn round and look us in the face: "What are you looking for?" he asks, "What do you want?" The question challenges us, and we find we are somewhere between the hope for a fine day and a wages settlement that was preoccupying us before we began, and the overflowing love of Christ that will fill us if we spend long enough with him in prayer. We are caught at the moment when we are beginning to feel our way to a deeper want than we were aware of before, a desire to be with Christ.

So in one way or another, verbally, imaginatively, physically, intellectually, with whatever faculties are operating at the time, we say to Christ, "I want to be with you. Let me follow you and spend this time with you, and then perhaps I will begin to understand what it is that I really want."

The whole purpose of the Spiritual Exercises can be summed up in terms of the *id quod volo*: the Exercises are a way through which we find out for ourselves what it is that we want most deeply.

For everyone, ultimately, the answer is the same. We want God, because that is the way we have been made. "You have made us for yourself, and our hearts find no peace until they rest in you" (see p. 18). But this answer takes on different aspects at different times. That is why this Third Prelude can also be called "the prayer for particular grace" – particular because it changes according to the subject matter: joy with Christ in joy, sorrow with Christ in sorrow.

We let Christ question us from out of the mystery that we

are contemplating: if we are with him in the stable we can let the baby in swaddling clothes challenge us; if we are with him at his Last Supper we can let the Lord who is about to be betrayed turn and put the question; if we are before him on the cross we let the crucified Jesus ask us what we want as we look at him.

The terms in which we express our wanting will also vary according to the person. One person's authentically felt desire may be "to give myself to God"; another's "to become more Christlike"; another's "to do everything for the greater glory of God"; another's again, "to bear witness to the truth". These are not different aims, but one aim differently apprehended according to the way God speaks to each.

Many people, however, have used terms very similar to the phrase of Ignatius "an intimate knowledge of our Lord, who has become human for me, that I may love him more and follow him more closely". We may remember the song from *Godspell*:

Day by day, day by day,
oh dear Lord, three things I pray:
to see thee more clearly,
love thee more dearly,
follow thee more nearly, day by day.

It is based on a prayer of Saint Richard, that goes like this:

Thanks be to thee, Lord Jesus Christ,
for all the benefits and blessings which thou hast borne for me.
O most merciful Friend, Brother and Redeemer,
may I know thee more clearly,
love thee more dearly,
and follow thee more nearly.

We can also remember the title of the famous classic by Thomas à Kempis, *The Imitation of Christ*. Others talk of the *sequela Christi*, which is Latin for "the following of Christ". The words that Ignatius uses to express what we seek are therefore central to the tradition of Christian spirituality.

I used a story from the beginning of John's gospel, which illustrates symbolically the way we let Christ gently question us at the beginning of our prayer, "What do you seek?" But the question is a recurring one in the fourth gospel, and it always challenges the listener. It always serves to change the situation slightly, to move things on, just as it helped John the Baptist's disciples to commit themselves to going home with Jesus, and just as it helps us in prayer to discover some deep desires within us.

So, in the garden of Gethsemane, Jesus asks the band of soldiers come to arrest him.

> "Whom do you seek?" They answered him, "Jesus of Nazareth". Jesus said to them, "I am he." . . . .When he said to them, "I am he", they drew back and fell to the ground. Again he asked them, "Whom do you seek?" (John 18:4–7)

The answer to that question in Gethsemane led the soldiers to fall to the ground with awe and fear before the one that they sought.

Outside the empty tomb Jesus puts the same question to Mary Magdalene:

> "Woman, why are you weeping? Whom do you seek?" Supposing him to be the gardener, she said to him, "Sir, if you have carried him away, tell me where you have laid him, and I will take him away." Jesus said to her, "Mary." She turned and said to him in Hebrew, "Rabboni!" (which means Teacher). (John 20:15–16)

Mary finds the answer to the question changes subtly as she is forced to answer it. The one she is seeking – what she really wants – is not a dead body but a living Lord.

And so, as we let ourselves be challenged by Christ's question: "What do you want? What do you really want?", we find the answer changes slightly even as we answer, and that is the function of prayer, to lead us forward towards our ultimate purpose. We may, like the disciples, simply want to be with Jesus, getting to know him; or we may, like the soldiers, find ourselves forced to the ground in shame; or we may, like Mary Magdalene, cry out with surprise and joy, "Rabboni!", as we find ourselves face to face with the one we really desire. Whichever way it is, we will have made some progress by letting Christ ask us what we want.

As the prayer continues, our sense of what we want may deepen, clarify, or find new forms of expression. When we come to conclude our prayer with a colloquy (see pp. 82–6) a good way of approaching that is to ask ourselves the question: "In the light of the meditation I have made, how would I now answer the question: what am I seeking? How has this time of prayer changed my perception, and revealed something more of my desire?"

Points

In the quotation at the head of this chapter, three points are envisaged. Sometimes Ignatius suggests four points (237), sometimes five (69–70), sometimes six (181–3, 195–7), but three is the most common number. The first exercise of the first week has three points, so does the contemplation on the nativity, the contemplation on the incarnation, and the Two Standards exercise. Further to this, of the fifty-two mysteries given in a long list at the back of the book (261–312), forty-eight have three points. (One has two points, and four Ignatius never got as far as dividing into points.)

So what on earth is a point? One person, of no particular religious allegiance, trying to understand what I was on about, suggested the word "pointer" rather than "point", and it is a good rendering. One translator of the *Spiritual Exercises* called them "headings". Points, or pointers, or headings give us an idea of what to think about in our prayers. They are lines of thought that can be developed.

The basic idea is that if you are going to spend an hour over your prayer, by the time you have made a preparatory prayer, two or three preludes, and, at the end, a colloquy, then you will get through the development of approximately three lines of thought in the remaining time. Once seen in that way, an hour for prayer seems less horrific. There is quite a lot to keep you going for an hour. And, of course, you are unlikely to keep track of what you are doing or which point you are at before you reach the end, because you will be absorbed in prayer that makes you forget the structure, and that is good.

Points can be more rational, or more imaginative in form. In the mysteries at the back of the book, Ignatius simply divides them into three stages of the story. For example, for the marriage at Cana,

FIRST POINT. Christ our Lord and the disciples were invited to the marriage feast.
SECOND POINT. His mother calls attention to the shortage of wine, saying to Him, "They have no wine". She bids the servants, "Whatsoever he shall say to you do".
THIRD POINT. He changed the water into wine, "And he manifested his glory and his disciples believed in him." (278)

But in the body of the *Spiritual Exercises*, the three points are more often laid out along this pattern:

FIRST POINT. This will consist in seeing the persons. . . .
SECOND POINT. This is to consider, observe, and contemplate what the persons are saying. . . .
THIRD POINT. This will be to see and consider what they are doing. . . . (114–16)

After each of these "I will reflect on myself that I may reap some fruit." (114) This structure of seeing the people, hearing what they say, and considering what they do is a more imaginative approach.

The imaginative approach is most marked of all in the five points of the exercise on hell, where they correspond to the five senses, so that we are invited to see, hear, smell, taste and touch the fires, the tears, and the cries. Modern parallels, vivid to the twentieth-century mind, are to experience imaginatively with the five senses the gas chambers of the concentration camps, or the torture-rooms of police-states, or the nuclear holocaust. Any of these will bring us right up against the reality of evil, which is what hell is all about. Whether we believe hell exists or not will not matter.

Very approximately, a prayer time that works through rational points can be called a meditation, and a prayer time that works through imaginative points can be called a contemplation. In a meditation we are thinking, in a contemplation we are simply being there, absorbed in nothing more than gazing.

The "prayer of simple regard", of which some contemplatives speak, should be more ordinarily translated (from the French "simple regard") as the "prayer of just looking". What we are "just looking" at may be the dark and awesome mystery of God; but it may also, in Ignatian teaching, be an imaginative scene from scripture, in which God can be seen in the flesh and blood person of Jesus Christ. Contemplation then becomes something that anyone can do, but it is still contemplation for all that.

However, people use the terms "meditation" and

"contemplation" in different ways, and it is not even clear that Ignatius always uses them consistently, so it is unwise to make too sharp a divide between the two. What is important is to realize God has given us the faculties to pray in both kinds of way, and most often our prayer will have elements of both.

It does not much matter if we use three points or six, or one for that matter; nor if we divide them according to the imaginative use of our senses, or according to the rational activity of our mind. Ignatius is basically reassuring us of a sense of pacing in our prayer: we cannot spend an hour with an empty mind meditating on nothing, nor can most people spin out one single consideration to last them that long.

But again, on the other hand, if we use a mystery well, exploring it through different angles, we need not dry up in even an hour's prayer. If we find ourselves racing through more than four or five or six lines of thought in an hour, or wanting to move on to another mystery, we need to take stock and slow down. And if our prayer time is considerably less than an hour, say ten or fifteen minutes, then one point alone may be quite sufficient.

Colloquy

"Colloquy" is another technical term for something that we do without thinking. All it means is "talking with". Whenever we say anything to God, we are making a colloquy, though sometimes we run out of things to say very soon, so it is not much of a conversation. When we make a colloquy, however, at the end of an hour's prayer, there can be more to say.

The chances are that anyone who spend periods of time in prayer is automatically making colloquies at the end without noticing it. Before we end the prayer it is a natural instinct to gather together the strands of thoughts and make a final presentation of them to God. It is quite natural, too, to move from the meditation mode into the colloquy mode, and back again, at any moment in our prayer – without thinking twice about it.

If we are aware of this natural need to make a colloquy, we can give it more attention and develop it. We can notice how in speaking to God we are making an act of will (see p. 28) that balances the preparatory prayer and the prayer for what I want (Third Prelude) from the opening of our meditation. We begin to see how prayer can be an interplay of reflections and intentions that feed each other, or as Ignatius says

> We make use of the acts of the intellect in reasoning, and of the acts of the will in manifesting our love. (3)

We speak to God from where we are now, which will be a slightly different place from where we were when we began the prayer. We will have had ideas and feelings, or concerns will have risen up, or perhaps faded away.

If we are praying on scripture the natural thing is to make some link with the story we have read and the thoughts it has prompted. We could pray, for example, for Christ to heal us as he healed the ten lepers. We could ask for healing particularly for those parts of ourself that we have felt most in need of healing as we prayed over the story. We could pray for others in need, perhaps people we know who have come into our thoughts during the hour, perhaps people we do not know who are ill or in other ways marginalized. We could tell Jesus that we want to remember to thank him, to be like the one leper who came back. We could tell him what are the things we want to thank him for. Or we could tell him that we are not very good at thanksgiving, and that we do not feel as much gratitude as we should, because we are so concerned with the things that are wrong with our life and not aware enough of the things that are right. We could tell him that we have enjoyed being with him for this time, and now like the leper we have to go and get on with the business of life, but that we hope he will stay with us and that we will remember he is with us. Or we could tell him that we have not had much sense of his presence and in a way feel the lepers had it easier in that they could actually see and speak with him face to face. And so on.

It should be natural and honest. It should also be reverent, because it is God we are talking to, and we remember how Moses took off his shoes before the burning bush. But being reverent does not mean hiding our real feelings and saying instead the sort of things we think we are meant to say to God. To do that would be to attempt to hide our sinfulness and shortcomings from God, and pretend we are better than we are.

Ignatius describes the colloquy as a simple, trusting, even intimate conversation:

> The colloquy is made by speaking exactly as one friend speaks to another, or as a servant speaks to a master, now asking him for a favour, now blaming oneself for some misdeed, now making known one's affairs to him, and seeking advice in them. Close with an *Our Father*. (54)

Further on in the Spiritual Exercises Ignatius returns to an explanation of the colloquy. He describes it in similar terms, but this time brings out more clearly how much it picks up and develops the theme introduced in the earlier prayer for what I want (Third Prelude):

> Attention must be called to the following point which was mentioned before and in part explained. In the colloquy, we should talk over motives and present petitions according to circumstances. Thus we may be tempted or we may enjoy consolation, may desire to have this virtue or another, may want to dispose ourselves in this or that way, may seek to grieve or rejoice according to the matter that we are contemplating. Finally, we should ask ourselves what we more earnestly desire with regard to some particular interests. (199)

Colloquies need not be made to God alone. In Catholic tradition it is quite common to pray to other people who we believe to be with God in heaven. What we are asking is their prayers to God for us, because they have all eternity in which to present our requests, and can compensate for the inadequacies of our own prayers. Prayers to Mary, the mother of Jesus, are frequent, but we can also pray to a saint who means a lot to us, perhaps a patron saint, or a saint we admire.

Some people are not at all happy about praying to those who have died. According to sound Ignatian principles, if it does not help, leave it alone. But if it does help, use it.

One particular form of colloquy that involves praying to Mary, the mother of Jesus, is what Ignatius calls the triple colloquy. It goes like this:

COLLOQUY. A colloquy should be addressed to our Lady, asking her to obtain for me from her Son and Lord the grace. . . . Then I will say the *Hail Mary*.

SECOND COLLOQUY. This will be to ask her Son to obtain the same favours for me from the Father. Then I will say, *Soul of Christ*.

THIRD COLLOQUY. This will be to beg the Father to grant me the same graces. Then I will say the *Our Father*. (147)

The *Hail Mary*, the *Soul of Christ* and the *Our Father* are printed out on pp. 88–90.

It is important to realize that we do not ask Mary to give us anything on her own account: what we ask is for her to pray to God for us. This is called intercession. One reason for asking her for what is God's to give, when there is nothing lacking in God's care and concern for us, is that some people find it easier to talk to Mary. This may or may not be because they have an over- severe, over-distant, or over-masculine image of God, but if it helps to pray to Mary, then pray to Mary. It can touch something in us that we did not know was there.

If we do not feel an initial distaste for this triple colloquy, it is worth trying. People can be unexpectedly struck by the subtly different quality of their prayer to each person, and the build-up of making the same petition three times over in a slightly different form helps to make our prayer more insistent. If we really want the grace we are asking for, very much, then it makes sense to try all possible channels of prayer.

The graces that Ignatius feels moved to make the triple colloquy for are particularly difficult graces. He feels the need to stress that he really has a desire for them, precisely when many of his inclinations go the other way (see the *agere contra*, pp. 42–3). The triple colloquy can help us in areas of struggle. In the passage quoted from above, Ignatius is asking for the grace to be received in "the highest spiritual poverty . . . even in actual poverty" (147). At another time he uses a triple colloquy to ask for knowledge of and sorrow for his sins (63). A third instance of the triple colloquy is to ask the grace to respond fittingly to the passion (199).

If we do not like praying to anyone other than God, we can make a triple colloquy of another sort. We can experiment with addressing God the Father, then the Son, then the Holy Spirit (Ignatius suggests this too – 109). We may find we approach them in slightly different ways, and that can be profitable.

Closing

When we have said all we have to express for the time being, we draw our prayer to a close. Some may make the sign of the cross (just as they may have done to begin the prayer). Some may make a prostration. But one excellent way, that is the way Ignatius suggests, is to say the *Our Father*.

We usually have a sense of the inadequacy of our prayer, and indeed our prayer always is inadequate. What the *Our Father* does is to complete our prayer, because it is given us by Jesus himself and is the most perfect prayer we have. Anything important we have forgotten to say or omitted to ask for is there. We do not always pray it well, really understanding and meaning the petitions we make – high and difficult demands like "Your will be done", or "Your kingdom come". But the fact that we have said them at all is a sign of our desire to make our prayer more worthy of God.

The *Our Father* is itself in the form of a colloquy, so we may use it at the end of our own colloquy, and finish our prayer session on that note. But if we use another way of, as it were, signing off, the important thing is that we do close. Drifting in and out of prayer is good when we are praying in the midst of ordinary activities, but when we set aside time specially for God, we should know whether we are in prayer or not. Just as we try to begin well, we try to end well too, and, with whatever residual sense of incompleteness we have, we look forward in confidence to our next session with the Lord.

When the prayer is over we will get even more out of what has taken place if we make a review, and maybe write some notes. But this will be described in Chapter 7.

Some Prayers

Hail Mary

Hail Mary,
full of grace,
the Lord is with thee.
Blessed art thou among women,
and blessed is the fruit of thy womb, Jesus.
Holy Mary,
mother of God,
pray for us sinners,
now and at the hour of our death. Amen.

The first sentence of this prayer is the greeting by the angel Gabriel at the annunciation. Then we have the greeting by Elizabeth, when Mary goes to visit her cousin. The third sentence is the prayer that the Church adds to these verses from scripture.

Soul of Christ

Soul of Christ, sanctify me
Body of Christ, save me
Blood of Christ, inebriate me
Water from the side of Christ, wash me
Passion of Christ, strengthen me
O good Jesus, hear me
Within thy wounds, hide me
Permit me not to be separated from thee
From the wicked foe, defend me
At the hour of my death, call me
And bid me come to thee
That with thy saints I may praise thee
For ever and ever. Amen

Anima Christi, sanctifica me
Corpus Christi, salva me
Sanguis Christi, inebria me
Aqua lateris Christi, lava me
Passio Christi, conforta me
O bone Jesu, exaudi me
Intra tua vulnera, absconde me
Ne permittas me separari a te
Ab hoste maligno, defende me
In hora mortis meae, voca me
Et iube me venire ad te
Ut cum sanctis tuis laudem te
In saecula saeculorum. Amen.

This prayer is placed by Ignatius at the beginning of the Spiritual Exercises, and though he did not invent it (we do not know who did) he certainly popularized it. Some people know it best in the hymn version, Soul of my Saviour, sanctify my breast.

Our Father

Our Father in heaven,
hallowed be your name,
your kingdom come,
your will be done,
on earth as in heaven.
Give us today our daily bread.
Forgive us our sins
as we forgive those who sin against us.
Lead us not into temptation
but deliver us from evil. Amen

This version comes from the Alternative Service Book, though most will be more familiar with the version that has "thy" and "trespasses". I have omitted the final doxology used by some, "For the kingdom, the power, and the glory are yours, now and for ever": although ancient it is not part of the prayer given us by Jesus in the gospels.

5

Reading, Meditating, Praying

One may kneel or sit, as may be better suited to our disposition and more conducive to devotion. We should keep our eyes closed, or fixed in one position without permitting them to roam. Then let us say, "Father", and continue meditating upon this word as long as we find various meanings, comparisons, relish and consolation in the consideration of it. The same method should be followed with each word of the Our Father, or of any other prayer which we wish to use for this method. . . . At the end of the prayer, we should turn to the person to whom the prayer is directed, and in a few words ask for the virtues or graces which we see we need most.

(Second Method of Prayer, 252, 257)

The last chapter spelt out the structure of a typical Ignatian hour in great detail. As we emphasized repeatedly, there is no need to remember all the steps or the order in which they come. The Ignatian plan may be helpful at the stage when prayer does not flow very naturally and an external framework provides support. Or it may be valuable to return to when one feels ready to explore in more detail some of the things one is doing instinctively, so as to understand them more deeply and develop them more fully.

This chapter covers essentially similar ground with a much simpler, three-part framework: reading, meditating, praying. This is so simple and so basic that for many people it is a much easier scheme to have consciously in mind while praying over scripture. It also forms an excellent guide for those unused to extended periods of meditation; they can go on to look at all the details of the Ignatian steps as they begin to feel at home with the practice.

"Reading, meditating and praying", or in Latin *lectio, meditatio, oratio*, forms a classic scheme of prayer known as *lectio divina*, or holy reading. It is the method developed and perpetuated by Benedictines, and it reaches right back to the ancient Church. As an explicit scheme we usually date it to St Benedict in the sixth century.

Not only is *lectio divina* of great antiquity, but it has provided the backbone for all teaching of scripture-based prayer ever since, so fundamental is it. There is an excellent explanation of this "Benedictine Method", in *Sadhana* (Exercise 33). The Spiritual Exercises draw very importantly on this Benedictine tradition, even though they do not mention it by name.

One can say that the *lectio*, or "reading" part, corresponds to the First Prelude (the history); the *meditatio*, or "meditating" part, to the Second Prelude right on through the points; and the *oratio*, or "praying" part, to the colloquy. One can also see a non-scriptural equivalent of *lectio divina* in what Ignatius called "the Second Method of Prayer", which is given at the back of the Spiritual Exercises (249–57). The quotation at the head of this chapter comes from this Second Method of Prayer. (The First Method of Prayer will be dealt with on p. 158).

Texts from scripture

Ignatius reflects the tradition of *lectio divina*, firstly in his emphasis on scripture as the material for prayer; secondly in his repeated stress on long relishing and slow absorption; and thirdly in his reminders to speak to God about the thoughts that come to us as we meditate.

One slight difference is that Ignatius rarely talks of reading as such, but rather of recalling the history. The very simple reason for this is that Ignatius was working with people who, before the days of the printing press, would not have had their own Bibles in the way we take for granted today; he therefore normally envisages the giver of the Exercises repeating the story from scripture, and the retreatant recalling it from memory.

Of course the early Benedictine monks did not have printing presses either, but since they were the chief copiers of manuscripts, the books of the Bible were part of the normal equipment of a monastery in a way that did not apply to the lay people and students among whom Ignatius was working.

Now that printed Bibles are so easy to get hold of (except in some parts of Eastern Europe) it is standard Ignatian practice to read the passage from scripture rather than just call it to mind. People making the Exercises are told the one and only book they need is the Bible (certainly not the book of the *Spiritual Exercises*). The same applies if one is making isolated Ignatian exercises, rather than the full sequence in retreat.

The three steps of *lectio divina* go like this: choose a passage from scripture that is not too long, perhaps a psalm, perhaps a chapter from the New Testament. Read it slowly and reverently, perhaps a verse at a time, perhaps less. This is the *lectio*.

As you come to a phrase that begins to mean something, that touches you in some way, stop, and repeat it, over and over. Relish these words from holy scripture, let them sink into your subconscious, and become part of you. Take your time over this: you want to carry these words around with you for always. This is the *meditatio*.

When you have dwelt on the phrase for a while, let prayer arise out of you. Perhaps you will want to celebrate your love and enjoyment of God by making an act of praise. Perhaps you will want to ask for help and grace. Perhaps you will share a sense of struggle and confusion. Perhaps you will want to humble yourself before God and ask forgiveness. It may be a wordless prayer that comes up from within, or it may be a matter of saying something to God. But in some way you gather up what is going on within you and direct it towards God in prayer. This is the *oratio*.

When you have finished meditating and praying on the verse, you turn back to the text and continue with your reading, until you have another phrase which you can meditate on and pray out of. So the reading, meditating, praying sequence can continue for as long as you have time or inclination.

If we now look back at the way Ignatius lays out the Mysteries of the Life of Our Lord in sets of three points for prayer (these are found in a long list at the back of the *Spiritual Exercises*, 261–312, see pp. 79–80 of this book), we notice he is using the same method. The points lay the story out in three chronological steps, quoting the phrases from the gospel (directly or indirectly) that struck Ignatius as important; in this way a period of time is spent dwelling on one phrase after another.

When we have stayed with a phrase, savouring it in the presence of God, and enriching it with the associations and reflections that come from our own life, then that phrase becomes precious to us for always. We may forget the details of our meditation, but if it has once been special to us in prayer something of that specialness will remain for ever. In this way we build up a deep love of the scriptures, bit by bit, through the verses we cherish – a love that no one else can give us.

Although we use the word "praying" for the last part of *lectio divina* (what Ignatius would call the colloquy) the whole process is prayer in the broader sense. Reading can be a form of prayer, just as thinking and speaking can be forms of prayer, if we make them so.

St Benedict said *Oratio sit brevis et pura*: "Let the prayer be brief and pure." Though the time of meditation may be long, anything we say to God arising out of it will have a quality of simplicity. We prefer to listen to God than to make God listen to us. Throughout the Bible God is reproaching people for not listening to him; he does not complain that they do not speak to him.

Listening is more important than talking to God, yet if we do not join in the conversation at all it is probably a sign that we are not good listeners. The best counsellors say very little, yet they always give some indication that they have heard what their clients have been telling them. Similarly when we have listened attentively to God we will want to give a brief indication that we have received the message.

If we have been reading or meditating in a state of quiet receptivity, this "brief, pure" quality should come naturally. We are more likely to make long, eloquent speeches to God if we jump into prayer without preparation, when the rhythm of everyday work is still driving us towards high productivity. But the heart-felt, authentic prayer that comes from a genuinely reverent meditation may be as simple as a repeated "Come, Lord Jesus". We remember again the instruction of Jesus, "In praying do not heap up empty phrases" (Matthew 6:7).

Other texts

The same method of read, meditate, pray can be used with spiritual reading that is not from the Bible, or with set prayers. St Augustine, or Julian of Norwich, to take only two examples, have given us writings that are beautiful to dwell on and to savour, though there is always something special about using scripture because we regard it as the word of God.

Lectio divina is a good way, also, of reading poetry. Many poems, in any case, cannot be understood unless we read them at this very slow pace, with plenty of time for the allusions to work in us. That makes them excellent material for prayer.

Again, as Ignatius suggests in his Second Method of Prayer (see the head of this chapter) we can use the same method for a set prayer. The three prayers in the Appendix to Chapter 4 are very suitable for this: the *Hail Mary*, the *Soul of Christ* or the *Our Father* (253). There is no minimum to be got through and no need to finish the prayer before the end of the session:

> If in contemplation, say on the *Our Father*, we find in one or two words abundant matter for thought and much relish and consolation, we should not be anxious to go on, though the whole hour be taken up with what we have found. (254)

One woman spent several sessions of prayer just on the phrase "Let there be light" from the first chapter of Genesis.

All that we have said in the last few chapters about, for example, entering our place of prayer, choosing a helpful position, putting ourselves in the presence of God, using a visual focus or in some other way composing ourselves, and so on, apply to this method of reading, meditating and praying, just as they did when we were considering the parts of prayer broken down in more detail. The Second Method of Prayer gives a brief summary of these recommendations before beginning on the actual matter of the prayer (250–2). After all, *lectio divina* is not a different form of prayer from what we have already talked of, but rather a briefer way of conceptualizing what we do when we pray.

A variant on the Second Method of prayer is the Third Method of Prayer (258–60). Instead of staying with a phrase for as long you find fruit there, you go through a prayer with a regular, but very slow, rhythm. Ignatius suggests one word with every breath: the rhythm of our breathing provides a kind of inbuilt clock that we are aware of without having to open our eyes. But you could also take a line at a time and leave approximately half a minute before going on to the next line.

This Third Method picks up the tradition of rhythmic prayer, which has had an important place in both Christian and non-Christian spirituality. One of the Christian practices of rhythmic prayer is the litany (such as a litany of the saints: "St Mary Magdalene, pray for us. St John the Baptist, pray for us". etc). Then there is the rosary which, with its regular sequence of one *Our Father*, ten *Hail Mary*s, and one *Glory Be* is entirely repetitive in form, and so provides a measured space for meditation on Christian mysteries. The *kyrie eleison* ("Lord have mercy") is one of our most ancient prayers of repetition. And the great Orthodox prayer for constant repetition is the "Jesus Prayer", which some pious Orthodox say over and over in the midst of their daily life. It goes like this: "Lord Jesus Christ, son of God, have mercy on me, a sinner"; or more briefly, "Lord Jesus Christ, have mercy on me."

In recent years some Christians – particularly those influenced by the method of meditation taught by the Benedictine, John Main, who died in 1982 – have taken up the practice of saying a mantra, or repeated word. It could be *maranatha*, which is Hebrew for "Come, Lord"; or *Abba*, which is Hebrew for "Father"; or *kyrie eleison*, or some other word that invokes the help of God.

This has its roots in the east, particularly in Hinduism, and it has become popular in secular western society through the spread of TM (Transcendental Meditation). But traces of a mantra-type tradition can be found also in the fifth-century Christian writer John Cassian, and in one passage of the medieval, anonymous classic, *The Cloud of Unknowing*, where the author suggests the repetition of one little word like "love", or "God" (§7).

Another Christian tradition of repetitive prayer, that operates over a much longer cycle, is the singing of the psalter at the monastic office. Over a period of time this can provide conditions for savouring and relishing the verses of scripture similar to those we have observed in the slower-moving *lectio divina*. One friar said that as he sang the psalms over and over in choir, particular verses would speak to him, according to the joys or struggles of his life at the time, and the association would then stick to that verse "like honey", so that he could never sing the same psalm again without remembering something of why it meant so much to him.

Honey is an evocative image to use. Perhaps in the back of his mind was the passage from Psalm 19:

> The ordinances of the Lord are true,
>   and righteous altogether.
> More to be desired are they than gold,
>   even much fine gold;
> sweeter also than honey
>   and drippings of the honeycomb. (Psalm 19:9–10)

If the word of God is sweeter than honey, of course it will make sense to spend time enjoying its sweetness. When we come to our meditation with the expectation of savouring, as it were, the drippings of the honeycomb, then we truly come with heart and mind prepared.

Read, meditate, pray . . . The scheme is beautiful in its simplicity, and there is no temptation for us to fret about getting it all right, or getting it all in. And so, fittingly, this is a much shorter chapter than the last one. After we have read a lot about prayer and learnt a lot of new terms we can get spiritual indigestion. It can then be a very good thing to set it all aside for a while and recall to our minds just a three-word outline which does not distract our attention on the mechanics of the exercise, but leaves our concentration free for God. Read, meditate, pray . . . "O taste and see that the Lord is good!" (Psalm 34:8)

Some texts for *lectio divina*

John's Prologue

In the beginning was the Word,
and the Word was with God,
and the Word was God.
He was in the beginning with God;
all things were made through him,
and without him was not anything made that was made.
In him was life,
and the life was the light of humanity.
The light shines in the darkness,
and the darkness has not overcome it.

There was a man sent from God, whose name was John.
He came for testimony, to bear witness to the light,
that all might believe through him.
He was not the light, but came to bear witness to the light.
The true light that enlightens every one was coming into
the world.
He was in the world, and the world was made through him,
yet the world knew him not.
He came to his own home, and his own people received
   him not.
But to all who received him,
who believed in his name,
he gave power to become children of God;
who were born,
not of blood nor of the will of the flesh nor of the will of
   a man,
but of God.

And the word became flesh and dwelt among us,
full of grace and truth. (John 1:1–14)

Psalm 84

How lovely is thy dwelling place,
   O Lord of Hosts!
My soul longs, yea, faints
   for the courts of the Lord;
my heart and flesh sing for joy to the living God.

Even the sparrow finds a home,
   and the swallow a nest for herself,
   where she may lay her young,
at thy altars, O Lord of hosts,
   my King and my God.
Blessed are those who dwell in thy house,
   ever singing thy praise!

Blessed are those whose strength is in thee,
   in whose heart are the highways to Zion.
As they go through the valley of Baca
   they make it a place of springs;
   the early rain also covers it with pools.
They go from strength to strength;
   the God of gods will be seen in Zion.

O Lord God of hosts, hear my prayer;
   give ear, O God of Jacob!
Behold our shield, O God;
   look upon the face of thine anointed!

For a day in thy courts is better
   than a thousand elsewhere.
I would rather be a doorkeeper in the house of my God
   than dwell in the tents of wickedness.

For the Lord God is a sun and shield;
   he bestows favour and honour.
No good thing does the Lord withhold
   from those who walk uprightly.
O Lord of hosts,
   blessed is the one who trusts in thee!

Hurrahing In Harvest

Summer ends now; now, barbarous in beauty, the stooks rise
   Around; up above, what wind-walks! what lovely behaviour
   Of silk-sack clouds! has wilder, wilful-wavier
Meal-drift moulded ever and melted across skies?

I walk, I lift up, I lift up heart, eyes,
   Down all that glory in the heavens to glean our Saviour;
   And, eyes, heart, what looks, what lips yet gave you a
Rapturous love's greeting of realer, of rounder replies?

And the azurous hung hills are his world-wielding shoulder
   Majestic – as a stallion stalwart, very-violet-sweet! –
These things, these things were here and but the beholder
   Wanting; which two when they once meet,
The heart rears wings bold and bolder
   And hurls for him, O half hurls earth for him off under his feet.
(Gerard Manley Hopkins)

6

Contemplating

This is to smell the infinite fragrance, and taste the infinite sweetness of the divinity. (124)

We cannot go far in our exploration of prayer before we find some very physical, sensual imagery cropping up. The last chapter ended with metaphors of tasting the Lord, and the sweetness of honey dripping from the honeycomb.

The texts that followed in the appendix also threw up some very vivid images. The psalm conjures up pictures of sparrows and swallows building nests round God's altars, and of springs and pools of rainwater refreshing a valley. John's Prologue speaks of the light shining in the darkness. The Hopkins sonnet brings to our eyes wild meal-drift being blown across the skies and violet hills. This last is less surprising: we are used to poems being rich in imagery, but we are less accustomed to thinking of prayer in general as something that belongs in the same, rich world of the imagination.

Even people who speak of prayer in very pure, mystical terms, are driven to the most physical metaphors to express the experience.

"Prayer can be like a slow interior bleeding, in which grief and sorrow make the heart's-blood of the inner person trickle away silently into our own unfathomed depths" (Karl Rahner, *Encounters with Silence*, p. 22).

Prayer is when "we taste the full bitterness of what we are. 'Our God is a consuming fire', and my filth crackles as he seizes hold of me; he 'is all light' and my darkness shrivels under his blaze" (Wendy Mary Beckett, "*Simple Prayer*", in *The Clergy Review*, February 1978).

Prayer is "a sharp dart of longing love", that smites "upon the thick cloud of unknowing" (*The Cloud of Unknowing*, 6).

Prayer is the entry into "a castle made of a single diamond or of very clear crystal, in which there are many rooms" (Teresa of Avila, *The Interior Castle*, 1).

Prayer is a "dark night", through which I go to a secret meeting with my lover; and "when the breeze blew from the turret, parting his hair, he wounded my neck" (John of the Cross, *The Dark Night of the Soul*, Stanzas of the Soul).

The last four, at least, of these writers are what could be called professional contemplatives. It almost seems true to say, the more contemplative the prayer is, the more bold and physical the images become. There is the gentleness of a breeze, and the fierceness of a crackling fire; there is the splendour of gleaming crystal, and the pain of interior bleeding.

All this physicality comes as a needed balance to the prevalent idea of contemplation as something almost impossibly empty and abstract. Far from being a blank and boring world, which we can admire from afar but refrain from entering for ourselves, we find it full of a life and richness that can only be explained, if at all, through concrete metaphors from the world of the senses.

In the last chapter we looked at the threefold sequence: *lectio, meditatio, oratio* or reading, meditation, prayer. Traditionally a fourth has sometimes been added to the series: *contemplatio*. We read, we meditate, we pray, and finally we contemplate. Contemplation is the climax of all prayer, in the sense that when we are "just looking" at God we really do not want to do anything else (see p. 81). So long as we are held in that moment of mutual presence, we neither want to vary our prayer, nor to leave it.

One of the most distinctive emphases of Ignatian teaching is its emphasis on the imagination as a way of entering contemplation. The techniques of imagination that Ignatius teaches are so simple that contemplation is put within the grasp of anyone. Even a child can do it; in fact we have to become something of a child to be able to do it, because adults tend to be a little inhibited. And yet it would be unjustified to represent this as a "Kontemplation for Kids" that necessarily bypasses the real experience. It can lead to very deep prayer indeed.

There are different kinds of contemplative prayer, and Ignatius himself uses the term in differing contexts. (The *Contemplatio ad Amorem*, for example, is not primarily based on the imagination, but on meditating on God's love: see Chapter 12.) The imaginative form of prayer is one of the ways, but not the only way, to contemplation, to this simple presence to God when we "just look". It is one of the easiest ways, one of the most effective, and one of which we find an echo, consciously or unconsciously, in almost any mystical writing in the Church's tradition.

We are probably already using our imagination to some extent when we pray, even if we have not been aware of it, and what Ignatius does is to help us notice, affirm and develop this faculty. Then we will not just be using physical imagery to describe our prayer experiences afterwards, but to help evoke them in the first place.

It is the fractional but decisive step of moving from a description of prayer, to an instruction on how to pray. Any of our mystical writers quoted above might have been capable of saying:

Prayer is the smelling of the infinite fragrance of the divinity.

Prayer is the tasting of the infinite sweetness of the divinity.

But Ignatius tells us not what he has done, but what we are to do. He gives us an imperative, telling us to

> smell the infinite fragrance, and taste the infinite sweetness of the divinity. (124)

Immediately contemplation moves from the realm of other people, into my own world.

Ironically Ignatius is just about the least poetic of any mystical writer who has ever lived. When he speaks of "the way from Bethany to Jerusalem, whether narrow or broad, whether level, etc.", no one is going to go away fired with inspiration.

But when we go away and pray on that road for ourselves, then the whole story becomes alive. We imagine that we see with our own eyes the road that Jesus travels on for the last time, as he approaches Jerusalem for his death, and we find ourselves travelling on it along with him. Whenever we call to mind again our image of that road, we will remember how it felt to be close to Jesus when he was drawing near to his death.

We use our imagination because it enriches and deepens our prayer, following the rule: use what helps. This is not cheating, but rather accepting the gifts God has made available to us. But of course the aim is not simply to have a rich fantasy life, nor to be so taken up in the sequence of activity that we do not stop to stand and stare, savouring the Lord's presence. If the imagination does not help us *pray*, if it does not deepen in us the desire to know God, love God and serve God, then there is no point in it.

Some people are bothered by the fact that their imagination will inevitably be historically inaccurate. This is to miss the point, for as explained above in the section on composition of place (pp. 70–4), it does not matter what the details are, so long as there are details and so long as they come up, without being forced, in the course of our prayer.

It is similar to the principle that makes the novel a work of art. When we read a story of love or suffering, of hope or failure, we often feel we are in touch with truth even though it is fiction. We may even weep at what we read, and it is a complete irrelevance if someone points out that the characters never existed and the events never happened. The truth is more real than if we had read a philosophical or a psychological treatise on these themes, because the novel is saying something not so much about the particular characters as about what it means to be human.

In the same way, when we imagine ourselves present on the road to Bethlehem, or at the lakeside, or in the empty tomb, we are in touch with truth no matter how differently different people envisage these places. Our images are communicating to us something, not about particular geographical locations, as about what it means for God to become human. Prayer of this sort will reach deeper inside us than any number of abstract theological propositions.

One moving example of this came when a young mother prayed over the nativity using the methods of imaginative contemplation: she saw that the hands of the baby Jesus were formed similarly to her own and her own daughter's. Whatever the real, historical shape of Jesus' hands, she was contemplating the truth of the incarnation, and seeing pictorially how God was born into the human family as her brother.

Imaginative exercises not from scripture

We saw in the section on composition of place how natural it is for images to form in our mind, whether we are praying on scripture or not, and how these act as a focus for our prayer. We might see ourselves before a sunset, or before a pool of water. We might hear the song of heavenly choirs, or we might by contrast feel ourselves impeded and weighed down by chains (74). There is really no end to the variety of images that in one way or another can serve the purposes of prayer, and the series of metaphors at the beginning of this chapter is witness to their power (bleeding, burning, a dart smiting a cloud, an interior castle, a meeting with a lover in a dark night, and so on). Some come from within us without prompting, others at the suggestion of perhaps a psalm or other passage from scripture.

Before going on to the full development of imaginative contemplation as a technique of scriptural prayer, it will be useful to look at some other types of prayer exercise that depend on a creative use of fantasy.

Sometimes Ignatius uses meditations that are built on thoughts and pictures of his own, rather than on a particular passage of scripture. These are sometimes known as the "key meditations". The Kingdom Exercise (91–8) is one of these, and we will look at it more closely at the end of Chapter 9. Another is the Two Standards (136–48), and we will look at this exercise now, for it is full of uninhibited flights of fantasy.

The two standards refer to two flags, and the whole scene is conceived in terms of two rival armies. We have to remember Ignatius' military background – he was using imagery that came naturally to him, but it could be problematic for us. It may be more helpful for us to think of another analogy for the two groups – two political parties, perhaps, or two rival businesses. But it is worth recounting Ignatius' exercise as it stands to show how dramatically the imagination can work in prayer.

The theme of the meditation is that Christ calls and wants us under his standard (or flag) while Lucifer wants us under his. (This is the First Prelude.)

107

We envisage two great plains: one, round Jerusalem, is the camp of Christ, who is "sovereign Commander-in-Chief of all the good"; the other plain, round Babylon, is the camp of Lucifer, the enemy. (This is the Second Prelude.)

The purpose of the exercise is to ask for the grace to know "the deceits of the rebel chief and help to guard myself against them; and also to ask for a knowledge of the true life exemplified in the sovereign and true Commander, and the grace to imitate Him". (This is the Third Prelude.)

First of all we imagine the fearsome enemy chief, "seated on a great throne of fire and smoke, his appearance inspiring horror and terror". He "summons innumerable demons, and scatters them" throughout the world until no individual is overlooked. He "goads them on to lay snares for people and bind them with chains".

Now the really serious point begins, for which all this visual extravagance has been nothing more than a setting:

> First they are to tempt them to covet riches . . . that they may the more easily attain the empty honours of this world, and then come to overweening pride.

> The first step, then, will be riches, the second honour, the third pride. From these three steps the evil one leads to all other vices. (142)

After Lucifer we turn to Christ. We see him standing on the plain round Jerusalem, "his appearance beautiful and attractive". Instead of demons, he sends "apostles, disciples etc.," throughout the whole world. The important part is this: that they are to help people by

> attracting them to the highest spiritual poverty, and . . . even to actual poverty. Secondly, they should lead them to

a desire for insults and contempt, for from these springs humility.

Hence, there will be three steps: the first, poverty as opposed to riches; the second, insults or contempt as opposed to the honour of this world; the third, humility as opposed to pride. From these three steps, let them lead people to all other virtues. (146)

Whatever reactions one may have to this imagery, we can recognize how it makes a powerful visual context for reflecting on the alternative syndromes of riches-honour-pride and poverty-insults-humility. It enables the meditation to be not just an intellectual exercise, but to be associated with images of great vividness that fix it in our minds. Lucifer is alarming and devious, Christ attractive and quietly authoritive.

Whether one makes the Two Standards as an imaginative exercise or not, it is valuable to reflect on these two sequences, riches-honour-pride and poverty-insults-humility – perhaps to see how they have been lived out in one's own life. One prisoner who made the exercise came to realize that most sin is associated with possessions. A woman who had worked in a community for the handicapped noticed how what she had most valued from that experience was the economy of possessions, the openness to criticism and the lack of any pretentiousness.

Following his founder, the Jesuit Anthony de Mello has a whole section on fantasy exercises in his book *Sadhana*. Exercise 16, for example, helps us to create a prayerful environment in our imagination even if (as envisaged on p. 29) we are actually in, say, an underheated house in a noisy street in a dirty slum.

We quieten ourselves and then remember or create a lovely

scene in which we can feel close to God – perhaps "a silent church, a terrace that gives on to the starry sky, a garden flooded by the light of the moon". We see it in as much detail as possible, notice the colours, hear the sounds – "the waves, the wind in the trees, the insects at night". And when we have taken in all the scene we are ready to raise our hearts and say something to God.

Another imaginative exercise from *Sadhana* that is much practised is Exercise 19. This is designed to heal painful memories from our past life, by recalling them in our imagination; but as we relive the event we look for the presence of the Lord in it, maybe even as a character playing a role in the action rather than just a vague presence.

De Mello also gives a statue exercise (Exercise 23) in which we are helped to look at ourselves with detachment. I imagine a statue of myself made by a sculptor, which I survey from all angles. I notice how I feel about it. Then I become a statue, and Jesus comes into the room and talks to me. Through an exercise like this (which is recounted in much greater detail in the book) it often happens "that your relationship with God has deepened, though you cannot explain why".

One of the most astonishing exercises in *Sadhana* is a meditation on my own corpse (Exercise 29). This comes from a buddhist series of reality meditations, and what is amazing is that, however horrifying it sounds in prospect, it gives a deep sense of peace.

There are nine stages: first you see your corpse cold and rigid, then turning blue, then cracks appear in the flesh, then decomposition sets in in some parts, then the whole body is in full decompostion, then the skeleton appears with some flesh adhering in some places, then there is the skeleton with no flesh left, then there is a heap of bones, lastly there is a handful of dust.

There is enormous scope for using the imagination in

prayer in ways like this; some people will find these exercises helpful, others may not. But the most characteristic imaginative exercise in Ignatian spirituality is the gospel contemplation. This is such a rich tool for prayer that it would be a great pity to pass it by, even if you need a little practice before it feels natural and comes easily.

Imaginative contemplation of a gospel mystery

An imaginative contemplation is when we take a mystery from the scriptures, usually from the life of Jesus, and pray our way through the events, as though we were there.

In the appendix at the end of this chapter are some gospel stories laid out in a form suitable for this style of imaginative contemplation. This exercise takes quite a while, and you will probably find you will be spending half an hour or so on one of these developed scenes. There is no need to work from one of the given examples: the method is easy and you can do it for yourself on any gospel passage you choose.

Some people take to this use of the imagination readily; others think they have no imagination, and can feel discouraged. But with some practice they can usually begin to notice the ways in which they are using images without realizing it. If they can relax the images will come more freely.

It is worth taking time to develop this facility, because the imaginative potential of prayer is so rich. But it is never a matter of forcing ourselves, rather of accepting what is given to us. If we are told to see the road and nothing comes it is better to go on to the next bit rather than devise a road in our intellect and then try to feed it into our imagination.

We noticed in the section on points (p. 81) how, having once set the scene of a mystery in the composition of place, we can turn our attention particularly to seeing the people, to hearing what they say, and to noticing what they do. Ignatius gives us an example of how this can work out, when he suggests that in the nativity contemplation

> I will make myself a poor little unworthy slave, and as though present, look upon them, contemplate them, and serve them in their needs with all possible homage and reverence. (114)

How much more will we be touched by the presence of the Christchild, if we see ourselves as a real character in the action, perhaps kneeling on the muddy straw, perhaps feeling the rough wood of the manger, perhaps close enough to hear the tiny sound of the baby's breathing, rather than floating around in the air in some unidentifiable way.

By asking myself "Where am I in this scene?" we find a great deal revealed about our relationship with God, and can use that knowledge to make progress. Here is one example of how this happened for one man, again using the nativity scene:

> A man who had been unable to pray for years began a retreat by imagining himself at Bethlehem but found he could not enter the cave. Feelings of unworthiness, and of simply not being welcome, blocked his fantasy at that point. He and his director interpreted this, not as an inability to "make the contemplation", but as a sign that he *was* praying; and he continued to imagine himself barred at the entrance to the cave in his repetitions of the contemplation. After two days of this, during which the resentments and hopes of his whole past life welled up within him, he reported that he was *invited* to go in. The fantasy, with the block and its resolution, was so much the man himself that it became the carrier for a real encounter and meant the turning point of his spiritual life. (Robert Ochs,

God is more present than you think, p. 62, Paulist Press, New York, 1970)

"Where am I?" is the question we ask when we have already begun to be present at the event. We do not decide where we should be, but notice where our perspective actually comes from when we look towards the Lord. Am I close to Jesus, or distant? Can I see his face, or am I behind his back? Am I one of the disciples? Perhaps someone who is addressed by Jesus, or healed by him? Or am I on the edges of it all, uncommitted but none the less interested?

Another way of developing the relationship between myself and Jesus is to see him turning to me after the main event recorded in the gospel. For example, after watching Jesus heal Jairus' daughter, we might let him turn to me and say something. Does he perhaps ask why I laughed (Luke 8:53)? Or does he ask me if I need healing? Or does he tell me I will see greater wonders than this? The imagined event can help us find out how we might respond if we met Christ face to face.

Apart from the question "Where am I in this mystery?" the main technique of imaginative contemplation is to go through the five senses. What do I see? What do I hear? What do I smell and taste? And what am I touching? This systematic exploration of my imaginative senses is called the "application of the senses" (121–6). Prayer of this kind is a matter of involved presence.

The last three senses – smell, touch and taste – sound as though they will be difficult but in fact turn out to be extraordinarily powerful. Some have said that you are really practising imaginative contemplation when you can feel the sand between your toes.

One man who prayed over the passage about the miraculous catch of fish – when Peter "fell down at Jesus' knees, saying, 'Depart from me, for I am a sinful man, O Lord'" (Luke 5:8) – found himself kneeling before Jesus, clutching the rough cloth of Jesus' robe between his fingers, smelling and tasting the salt wind from the sea. That incident remained for him a key moment of his retreat. Someone else who prayed over Palm Sunday could smell the scent of the donkey, and feel its rough coat under her fingers. A woman who prayed over the agony in the garden found the sweet smell of the evening air among the olive trees an evocative memory. Someone who prayed over the breakfast by the lakeside, in the last chapter of John, could taste the crusty brown bread and the smoky flavour of the grilled fish.

When we have prayed over a gospel mystery with our imagination, we will find that we have built up a memory that lasts for us, just as our own life experiences live on in our memories. Whenever we read that mystery again, or even hear it mentioned, we will have a sense of "I know that occasion: I was there". We may feel nostalgia, or at any rate a reflection of the feelings we had when we prayed over it. The gospel events will become my memories, part of the stock of memories that make me who I am. Over a lifetime we can build up a huge stock of gospel memories.

This makes a lot of sense when we reflect that the stories we have in the scripture are not brute fact, in any case, but people's memories. We recall how Jesus' mother, Mary, "kept all these things in her heart" (Luke 2:51). Biblical scholars are always quick to point out that the gospel stories are not accurate historical records. Because they are memories they are selective, and different evangelists may focus on and recall different parts of the conversations or events, according to what seemed important to them or their sources at the time. When we pray over these same stories with our imagination we are taking part in the same process. We are taking other people's memories, and through our own work of appropriation we make them our own memories.

The inaccuracies of our version will not matter any more

than the inaccuracies of the gospels matter, because they will be inaccuracies about incidentals rather than essentials. It does not matter if Jesus declared the Beatitudes sitting on the mount, or if there was one angel or two in the empty tomb: what matters is that the sermon is a true reflection of Jesus' moral teaching, and that he rose from the dead. And it also matters that we should have some way of making this a living truth for ourselves and not just a bit of theory.

This imaginative method of Ignatius is a traditional Christian practice, though often instinctive rather than consciously developed. We can find traces of it throughout our devotional literature. For example, in the famous Latin hymn, the *Stabat Mater*, we are given a glimpse of the way in which Mary, the mother of Jesus, stood at the foot of the cross, silently and steadily watching, as though we ourselves were there seeing her.

> O that silent, ceaseless mourning,
> O those dim eyes, never turning
>   From that wondrous, suffering Son.
> Who on Christ's dear Mother gazing,
> In her trouble so amazing,
>   Born of woman, would not weep?

Or, to take just one more example, the ancient Latin hymn on the resurrection *Victimae Paschali Laudes*, imaginatively reconstructs a fragment of the conversation of Mary Magdalene with the other disciples after her visit to the empty tomb.

> "Speak Mary, declaring
> What thou sawest wayfaring:"
> "The Tomb of Christ, who is living,
> The glory of Jesus's Resurrection:
> Bright angels attesting,
> The shroud and napkin resting."

The application of the senses is so intimate and powerful a form of prayer that, in the classic scheme of the Ignatian retreat, Ignatius treats it as the climax of the day. Four hours will have been spent praying over either one or at the most two mysteries, from various angles, with the help particularly of the senses of sight and hearing; but the fifth, and last hour of the day will be spent in the stillness of simple presence, not only seeing and hearing, but also smelling, tasting and touching (159).

We are most contemplative when these sense data focus us towards the Lord himself, in a quiet stillness where, to use Ignatius' word, we simply want to "relish" the presence of Christ:

> In making the Application of the Senses, attention and more time is to be given to the more important parts and to points where the soul was more deeply moved and spiritual relish was greater. (227)

This is the context in which Ignatius speaks of smelling "the fragrance" and tasting "the sweetness of the divinity" (in the quotation at the head of this chapter). He also speaks of "embracing and kissing the place where the persons stand or are seated, always taking care to draw some fruit from this" (125).

St Anthony of Padua did something similar to this when he held the Christchild in his arms and felt his fragility. Julian of Norwich saw and smelled with her inner senses when she "saw the red blood trickle down from under the garland, hot and fresh and plentiful" (*Showings*, 4). Ignatius himself experienced God with the ears of his soul when he had a vision of the Trinity as a chord of three notes.

Two beautiful passages from Augustine's *Confessions* go

through all five senses as a way of describing the wonder of the divinity. One of these continues a quotation that we began to look at on p. 33. Lovely as creation is, God is lovelier still to hear, see, smell, taste and touch.

> You called me; you cried aloud to me; you broke my barrier of deafness. You shone upon me; your radiance enveloped me; you put my blindness to flight. You shed your fragrance about me; I drew breath and now I gasp for your sweet odour. I tasted you, and now I hunger and thirst for you. You touched me, and I am inflamed with love of your peace. (*X.27*)

The other passage, from the same book of the *Confessions*, calls up the most sensuous experiences to evoke the enjoyment of God. We can just read this as a piece of abstract theology, but if instead we call up imaginatively the sensations Augustine describes and pray with the text, we can uncover a deep desire for God within us – the God who is infinite satisfaction to all of these appetites, and more.

> But what do I love when I love my God? Not material beauty or beauty of a temporal order; not the brilliance of earthly light, so welcome to our eyes; not the sweet melody of harmony and song; not the fragrance of flowers, perfumes, and spices; not manna or honey; not limbs such as the body delights to embrace. It is not these that I love when I love my God. And yet, when I love him, it is true that I love a light of a certain kind, a voice, a perfume, a food, an embrace; but they are of the kind that I love in my inner self, when my soul is bathed in light that is not bound by space; when it listens to sound that never dies away; when it breathes fragrance that is not borne away on the wind; when it tastes food that is never

consumed by the eating; when it clings to an embrace from which it is not severed by fulfilment of desire. This is what I love when I love my God. (*X.6*)

Some contemplations

The Marriage At Cana: John 2:1–12

Become quiet in the presence of God.
Cast an eye over the whole passage, without delaying over it,
to recall the overall shape of the story.

*On the third day there was a marriage at Cana in Galilee, and the
mother of Jesus was there; Jesus also was invited to the marriage, with
his disciples. When the wine gave out, the mother of Jesus said to him,
"They have no wine". And Jesus said to her, "O woman, what have you
to do with me? My hour has not yet come". His mother said to the
servants, "Do whatever he tells you". Now six stone jars were standing
there, for the Jewish rites of purification, each holding twenty or thirty
gallons. Jesus said to them, "Fill the jars with water". And they filled
them up to the brim. He said to them, "Now draw some out, and take it
to the steward of the feast". So they took it. When the steward of the feast
tasted the water now become wine, and did not know where it came from
(though the servants who had drawn the water knew), the steward of the
feast called the bridegroom and said to him, "Everyone serves the good
wine first; and when people have drunk freely, then the poor wine; but
you have kept the good wine until now". This, the first of his signs, Jesus
did at Cana in Galilee, and manifested his glory; and his disciples
believed in him. After this he went down to Capernaum, with his mother
and his family and his disciples; and there they stayed for a few
days.*

Ask God's grace, to come to know Jesus better through
contemplating the mystery of the marriage at Cana; and
through knowing him better, to love him more and be a better
follower. Then go through the passage again slowly like this:

1–2. On the third day there was a marriage at Cana in Galilee, and the mother of Jesus was there; Jesus also was invited to the marriage, with his disciples.

Is the wedding feast inside or out of doors?
See the surroundings.
See the guests, the tables.
Smell the food.
Is there music? dancing? other entertainment?
Are there children? What are they doing?
See the bride and groom.
See Mary. See Jesus. See his disciples.
Where am I? Who am I? What am I tasting?

3. When the wine gave out, the mother of Jesus said to him, "They have no wine".

Can I hear her say it? Can others hear her say it?
How does she say it, and how does she look?
Can I sense her concern at why it is important to have more wine?

4. And Jesus said to her, "O woman, what have you to do with me? My hour has not yet come!"

Can I hear him say it? Can others hear him say it?
How does he say it, and how does he look?

5. His mother said to the servants, "Do whatever he tells you."

How does she say it?
See the servants. How many? young or old? Where am I? Am I a servant?

6. Now six stone jars were standing there, for the Jewish rites of purification, each holding twenty or thirty gallons.

See the jars. What is their shape? colour? texture? Can I feel them? Where are they?

7. Jesus said to them, "Fill the jars with water." And they filled them up to the brim.

Where is Jesus standing now? How does he say it?
Where am I? Do I see this scene, or is it recounted to me by another?
Can I see them fill the jars up? How do they do it? Does it take long?
Can I hear the water being poured?

8. He said to them, "Now draw some out, and take it to the steward of the feast." So they took it.

Can I hear him say it? Can I see it? Can I smell the new wine?

9–10. When the steward of the feast tasted the water now become wine, and did not know where it came from (though the servants who had drawn the water knew), the steward of the feast called the bridegroom and said to him, "Everyone serves the good wine first; and when people have drunk freely, then the poor wine; but you have kept the good wine until now."

Do I see this scene, or is it recounted afterwards?
How do I feel when I hear this comment?
Do I want to tell him who Jesus is?
Do I taste the new wine, too? Can I smell its bouquet? Can I see it in the wine glass?

FINDING GOD IN ALL THINGS

11–12. This, the first of his signs, Jesus did at Cana in Galilee, and manifested his glory; and his disciples believed in him. After this he went down to Capernaum, with his mother and his family and his disciples; and there they stayed for a few days.

Do I come to believe in him during this feast? If I already believed in him, does it strengthen my faith? Do I have a sense of Christ's glory manifested?

Do I go with him down to Capernaum? How does the memory feel during the following hours and days?

What can I learn about my relationship with Jesus, from where I found myself in this scene?

What do I want to say now, before I finish my prayer? Who do I want to say it to? to Jesus? Or to his Father? Or to Mary?

The Anointing at Bethany : Mark 14:3–10

Become quiet in the presence of God.
Cast an eye over the whole passage, without delaying over it, to recall the overall shape of the story.

And while he was at Bethany in the house of Simon the leper, as he sat at table, a woman came with an alabaster flask of ointment of pure nard, very costly, and she broke the flask and poured it over his head. But there were some who said to themselves indignantly, "Why was the ointment thus wasted? For this ointment might have been sold for more than three hundred denarii, and given to the poor." And they reproached her. But Jesus said, "Let her alone; why do you trouble her? She has done a beautiful thing to me. For you always have the poor with you, and whenever you will, you can do good to them; but you will not always have me. She has done what she could; she has anointed my body beforehand for burying. And truly, I say to you, wherever the gospel is preached in the whole world, what she has done will be told in memory of her." Then Judas Iscariot, who was one of the twelve, went to the chief priests in order to betray him to them.

Ask God's grace, to come to know Jesus better through contemplating the mystery of the anointing at Bethany; and through knowing him better, to love him more and be a better follower.

3a. And while he was at Bethany in the house of Simon the leper, as he sat at table . . .

What sort of a house does Simon the leper have in Bethany?
See the room. How many people are at table?
Are there others around, perhaps coming in and out?
How do you see Simon the leper? In Luke's account of the anointing (which some people think is the same, others a

different event) the host is a Pharisee called Simon; do you
see Simon the leper as a Pharisee?
Where is Jesus?
Where am I?

*3b. . . . .a woman came with an alabaster flask of ointment of pure
nard, very costly, and she broke the flask and poured it over his head.*

Watch the woman come in. What does she look like? How
does she behave?
In Luke's account she is a sinner; in this account do you see
her as a sinner?
See the alabaster flask; its shape; its size; its colour; its
texture. If you touch it, how does it feel? How does the
woman carry it?
Watch the woman break the flask. Does it make a noise?
Watch the ointment pour out. Can you smell it? What is the
consistency and colour of the ointment?
See the ointment being poured on Jesus' head. How does he
respond? Can I see the expression on his face?
Where am I now? (Am I the woman?)

*4–5. But there were some who said to themselves indignantly, "Why
was the ointment thus wasted? For this ointment might have been sold
for more than three hundred denarii, and given to the poor." And they
reproached her.*

See these people. (Am I one of them?)
Verse 10, below, will tell us that Judas went to the chief
priests to betray Jesus after this incident; and in John's
parallel account this complaint is put in the mouth of Judas.
Can I see Judas among the reproachers?
See their expressions.

Can I hear them murmuring?
Can I hear them reproaching her? How do they behave towards her?

6. *But Jesus said, "Let her alone; why do you trouble her? She has done a beautiful thing to me. . . ."*

See and hear Jesus say this. Does he make any gesture at the same time?

7. *"For you always have the poor with you, and whenever you will, you can do good to them; but you will not always have me."*

Hear these words. What am I feeling as I hear them?

8. *"She has done what she could; she has anointed my body beforehand for burying."*

Hear Jesus say this. Do I understand what he means? What am I thinking?

9. *"And truly, I say to you, wherever the gospel is preached in the whole world, what she has done will be told in memory of her."*

How does Jesus say this? Have my feelings been altered by this speech by Jesus? Do I respond in any way?
Do I want to say anything back to Jesus? If I do speak, how does he answer me now?
How does the scene continue? Does the woman continue with her task? When she has finished, how does she leave? Where am I now? How am I feeling?

10. Then Judas Iscariot, who was one of the twelve, went to the chief priests in order to betray him to them.

It would take a whole new contemplation to see and hear this, but how does this grave outcome of the anointing at Bethany affect my feelings about what I have just lived through?

Could I feel the seriousness of the incident at the time?

Was I aware that the tension between Jesus and Judas was as critical as this?

Does this knowledge cast a shadow of pain back over my memory of the anointing? Or some other feeling?

What can I learn about my relationship with Jesus from this scene? Has my relationship altered in any way that I can point to?

What do I want to say to Jesus, or to his Father, before I finish my prayer?

The Mission Charge : Matthew 28:16–20

Become quiet in the presence of God.
Cast an eye over the whole passage, without delaying over it,
to recall the overall shape of the story.

*Now the eleven disciples went to Galilee, to the mountain to which
Jesus had directed them. And when they saw him they worshipped
him; but some doubted. And Jesus came and said to them, "All
authority in heaven and on earth has been given to me. Go therefore
and make disciples of all nations, baptizing them in the name of the
Father and of the Son and of the Holy Spirit, teaching them to observe
all that I have commanded you; and lo, I am with you always, to the
close of the age."*

Ask God's grace, to come to know Jesus better through
contemplating the mystery of the mission charge; and
through knowing him better, to love him more and be a
better follower.

*16. Now the eleven disciples went to Galilee, to the mountain to
which Jesus had directed them.*

This refers back to verse 10, when Jesus asked the women
who were his first Easter witnesses to go and tell his disciples
"to go to Galilee, and there they will see me." As I journey
there I remember being given this instruction.
Climb the mountain. What are my legs feeling like as I climb?
Do I have to look to see where to put each foot, or is the
ascent gentle?
See the whole mountain. See the view. Notice the sky and
the weather.
What other sensations do I have? (Heat from the sun? A
wind?)

See the rest of the group. Are there just the eleven disciples,
or others as well?
Do they travel in a close group, or scattered? Do they talk, or
are they silent?
Where am I in the group? Am I anyone in particular?
How am I feeling?
Am I making an act of commitment in going? or am I going
out of curiosity?

17. *And when they first saw him they worshipped him; but some
doubted.*

I catch my first glimpse of Jesus.
How far away is he? What does he look like? Am I sure it is
him yet?
Approach Jesus, seeing him gradually come closer.
As I draw nearer I register more exactly the details of the
place.
What noises can I hear on the mountain? (wind, or birdsong
perhaps? distant noises? the breathing or talking of the dis-
ciples?)
What sort of terrain am I walking on? (grassy? stony? muddy?)
How is my body feeling?
What is the air like? (fresh mountain air? damp or dry?)

Now I am really close to Jesus. I see him more and more
clearly.
Some of the disciples are worshipping Jesus, some are not.
How do they show they are worshipping him?
Do I worship? Do I doubt? Is my reaction swift, or delayed?
What do I do?
Does Jesus look at me? If so, how?
How does Jesus respond to the group as a whole?

18. And Jesus came and said to them, "All authority in heaven and on earth has been given to me. . . ."

How close does Jesus come? Watch him come.
How do I feel at these words?

19–20a. ". . . . Go therefore and make disciples of all nations, baptizing them in the name of the Father and of the Son and of the Holy Spirit, teaching them to observe all that I have commanded you. . . ."

Hear Jesus say this.
Am I taking this as a personal charge to me, among others?
How am I feeling?

20b. ". . . . and lo, I am with you always, to the close of the age."

Hear the words. Look at Jesus as he says them.
How do they make me feel? Do I believe him?

How does the scene end? How does Jesus leave? Is this the moment when he ascends to heaven? (These are the last words of Matthew's gospel, so that could be a fitting ending.) What feeling am I left with after Jesus has gone?

What can I learn about my relationship with Jesus from this scene?
What do I want to say to Jesus, or his Father, before I finish my prayer?

7

Noticing What Happens

After an exercise is finished, either sitting or walking, I will consider for the space of a quarter of an hour how I succeeded in the meditation or contemplation. (77)

This chapter is about self-awareness. We need to foster the art of noticing what happens to us when we pray, and of noticing what happens to us in the way we live our lives. If we do not acquire habits of awareness, we will be unable to apply the Ignatian principles we have learnt, especially the Foundation principle: "use things in so far as they help, and avoid them in so far as they hinder". It does not say "use things in so far as you have been told they will help. . .", but presupposes an experimental approach in which we check our choices out against their effects. Reflection on experience provides the basis for ordering our life.

Whether through laziness or inherited legalism, we have a great capacity for failing to see the obvious.

> This people's heart has grown dull,
> and their ears are heavy of hearing,
> and their eyes they have closed,
> lest they should perceive with their eyes,
> and hear with their ears,
> and understand with their heart
> and turn for me to heal them.

(Matthew 13:15)

We frequently fail to make links of cause and effect that are really quite apparent if we pay a bit of attention. We let ourselves be swirled on in life as though by the current of a mighty river: there is always a new call on our attention, a new distraction. We do not stop to look.

Because of this human short-sightedness and rushing, it is necessary to discipline ourselves into habits of self-awareness. When we put aside a little time to look over our prayer and notice what is happening, we call it the review. When, according to similar principles, we put aside a little time to look over our daily life and notice what is happening, we call it the examination of consciousness (or the examen); this exercise will be given in the Appendix to Chapter 8.

In neither case is the initial focus on self-judgement, but on self-awareness. Too hasty self-criticisms of "I should have done this", "I should have done that" can actually block our awareness, because we do not give ourselves time and space to notice the effects of what we did do. If we can keep our attention on observation, the conclusions for our behaviour should be apparent enough.

Since the idea of reviewing is to notice whether our methods are working, we may need to experiment to find the best formula. Each of us has a personal way of relating to God. Each has a personal vocation. Similarly each will be helped by different devotional practices. There are guidelines from others, of course, but they need to be tested out in our own experience.

Ignatius explicitly recommends some systematic experimentation, in his sections on penance and fasting. "It is often useful to make some change," he says, "so that we alternate, for two or three days doing penance, and for two or three not doing any. The reason for this is that more penance is better for some and less for others." (89). The criterion for finding the right mean is, in typically Ignatian fashion, that it enables us to find what we are seeking – the *id quod volo*.

The same principle can be applied to our use of prayer. By experimenting, and noticing the effects on us, we can reach an informed decision about questions like when?, where?, how long?, and what method? With our eyes on what we are looking for, we take all intelligent means to search out the best path with a certain amount of trial and error. But we remember also the rule that cuts out excessive dabbling in variety: when we are finding what we desire we stay with it, we make no change. Experiment is to help us find what we want, not to build up a research sheet of results.

The principal help to checking over our prayer and seeing if our approach is working for us, is the review.

Reviewing one prayer period

Anyone making the Spiritual Exercises as a formal retreat is asked to write down, for their own eyes, a short account of every prayer session they make. These notes form the basis for each session of spiritual direction with the retreat-giver. Over the course of the retreat they build up into a moving, spiritual journal, recording the ways in which God has touched us. Looking back over a journal afterwards we can be amazed at the depth and richness of what has been going on, much of which, without a record, we would have forgotten.

What is true of a whole retreat is also true, in a lesser degree, of every prayer time we spend outside of retreat. God gives us gentle, imperceptible graces, and if we do not train ourselves to notice what is happening, and to remember it, we may think nothing is going on and become discouraged.

It can be a good idea to keep a spiritual journal through any period when we are praying with some regularity. For example, some people make a special effort to pray regularly during Lent, and they may be helped by keeping a Lenten diary: it can give them a sense of going somewhere. Or you can keep a record of the prayer exercises you have tried from a book like *Sadhana*, or from this book for that matter: it can help you to see which would be the most profitable exercises to persist with and develop.

Whether we write down our reflections or not, it is good to recall them to mind, instead of closing the book on our prayer as soon as it is finished. Prayer is something to look forward to beforehand, to relish at the time, and to remember with pleasure afterwards, because prayer is what we choose to do because we love God. If we think of prayer as a duty, to be fitted in somewhere in the day because we have been told to do so, then we may breathe a sigh of relief when our time is up, and mentally switch off; and if we do that much of the fruit of our prayer is lost forever.

And so whether we think of it as a review in a formal sense or not, it is good to cast at least a brief reflective glance backwards, and to apply the general principle of noticing what happens when we pray.

The purpose of having the review time after the meditation is over, is to allow our prayer time to be spontaneous, so that we are not constantly checking over what we are doing while we are actually in prayer: that could make us too self-conscious and inhibit our relaxed receptivity to God.

Occasionally people find that the need to make a review afterwards has the opposite effect: they can be wondering what they are going to write at the end, so they try to have the right kind of thoughts. Or they are afraid that they will forget an idea, so in effect they make several reviews during the course of the prayer in case they cannot remember later. If you find that happening it may be better to forget about the review for a while, or try to reduce its importance in your mind. Or you could write down a very brief note – like a one-word reminder – to take away the anxiety about forgetting.

Some people find it more helpful to write things down as they go along. One woman spoke of the naturalness of "praying with a pen in hand". If this helps you pray, it must be good. But it could divert you into articulating thoughts, so always keep the aim of prayer uppermost.

Just as the preparation for prayer should be clearly distinguished from the prayer time itself, so that the two do not imperceptibly drift into each other, so the same is true for the review. When you have drawn the prayer to a close you can then scratch your nose, have a stretch, make a cup of tea if you like, and do a written or mental review in a less intense atmosphere. It is a good idea to do the review straightaway at the end if you can, because later in the day you will already have forgotten a great deal.

The classic Ignatian pattern is to take a quarter of an hour for review at the end of an hour's prayer. If you are writing notes you will probably find it takes that long. But if the prayer has been much less than an hour, or if you are simply remembering, and are not formally in retreat, then you may use much less.

In the review time you recall the course of your prayer, looking in particular for what was fruitful and also what was less successful. It should not have the flavour of hard work, but rather of happy memories.

The review has been described extremely simply in these terms: Where did I experience consolation? Where did I experience desolation? That is an excellent way of thinking about it, but since we have not yet examined the Ignatian terms "consolation" and "desolation" (see pp. 183–9) a rather longer explanation may be necessary at this stage.

The following list of questions is only suggested as a rough guide of the sort of thing I can be noticing. It would not normally be helpful to go through the list like a questionnaire. (On the contrary, one man said the review was rather like poetry, because you just jotted things down as they occurred to you.)

Did the prayer on the whole go well or badly? If well, let me give thanks for that, and share the enjoyment with God. If badly, was there some obvious reason over which I could have had some control? For example, was I too tired? Was the place I chose too noisy? Can I avoid these difficulties next time? Did I manage to enter into a prayerful disposition? If so, was there anything that I did to compose myself, that I could profitably use another time? If not, was it because I rushed into the session without a careful preparation? Might it be helpful another time to try spending a little longer opening myself up to God at the beginning, perhaps going through the Preludes?

What was the matter of my prayer? If I used scripture, how much did I get through? What insights did I have?

If I was not getting much out of it, was it because I was trying to go too fast? Or perhaps I took too little, and could have found more fruit if I had let my eye run on just a few verses more?

Was I hampered by textual obscurities, so that I might have been clearer if I had looked at a commentary first? Was I, on the other hand, over-concerned with academic questions, so that I was not touched at a personal level by the passage?

Was my prayer primarily a matter of thought, or of images? What ideas or sensations gave me the most satisfaction? Can I recall those thoughts or feelings, to cherish the grace and to thank God for it?

Was there anything in my prayer that disturbed me, or gave me a sense of discomfort? Do I understand why I was troubled there? Was there any point at which I seemed to come up against a block? Is there something here that needs looking at and working on?

Did I manage to address myself to God directly, with words or without words? When I stopped, was there still more that could be fruitfully explored? When do I plan to make my next prayer period? What would I like to use as material for that? Would it be a good idea to carry on with a theme that I have begun in this session?

It is important that we do not automatically blame every failure on ourselves. That would be a terrible mistake, because difficulties in prayer are often not our fault at all. It may simply be that the kind of prayer God chooses to give us for the time being is a dry form of prayer, because dry prayer has its own special value.

So we are not digging around for things to blame ourselves for; rather, with a simple, straightforward mind, we are observing what went on, and checking that we were not making matters unnecessarily difficult for ourselves.

When the prayer is good and rich, it is a real pleasure to recall the thoughts and images that gave us happiness. When we feel challenged by our prayer, and aware of our sinfulness, there is a satisfaction, making the review, in knowing that we are not running away from what God is showing us. Even when the prayer is dry, the review can help us feel better about it: we can recognize our difficulties and if we are writing notes we can express our frustration on paper.

If we write down, "14th October. Used feeding of five thousand. Nothing came. Was longing for the time to be up", we may feel rather better to have got that down. Having written that, we might then find that after all there had been a little insight here and a soft shadow of the love of God there, and we can write them down and probably find there was more there than we had realized – slight graces, half-hidden.

Often graces are like that – not the great, dramatic bangs that we want to be provided with so that we can be in no doubt of God's presence – but like little brush-strokes that need to be taken together before the picture is slowly built up.

Ignatius said that grace is "delicate, gentle, delightful. It may be compared to a drop of water penetrating a sponge" (335). It does not clang like "a drop of water falling upon a stone", and we may not notice it at all unless we have accustomed ourselves to look for its almost imperceptible action.

And yet, though it may feel at the time as though hardly anything is happening, I do not believe there is any human activity that yields more plentiful results in terms of time invested, than prayer. In no more time than it takes to have a bath, or to do the washing up, we can reshape our whole purpose in life, day by day, and fill ourselves with spiritual enrichment. What Jesus said about the kingdom of heaven is true about private prayer as a part of that kingdom.

> It is like a grain of mustard seed, which, when sown upon the ground, is the smallest of all the seeds on earth; yet when it is sown it grows up and becomes the greatest of all shrubs, and puts forth large branches, so that the birds of the air can make nests in its shade. (Mark 4:31–2)

Repetition

One of the points we may have considered in the review – or if not then we will consider it in our next preparation for prayer (see pp. 66–8) – is whether to return to the same material in a subsequent prayer session. I have frequently stressed how important it is in prayer not to rush ahead, but to stay, to ponder, to relish, to move slowly. By the same principle it is an excellent practice to return in prayer to where we were before, and go into still greater depth on the same passage or theme.

Ignatius calls this a "repetition", and it is a characteristic of his Spiritual Exercises that repetitions play a major part in the process.

A repetition is never simply repeating everything that you did before, which would be predictably tedious. Rather it is like a close-up of particular areas of the preceding prayer, where you feel the Spirit is leading you. Ignatius says that in a repetition

> attention should always be given to some more important parts in which one has experienced understanding, consolation, or desolation. (118)

Repetitions enable us to go into our prayer in greater depth, and to explore the message God has for us, in a particular mystery at a particular time, in greater fullness.

The review will help us to decide when to do repetitions, and where to focus those repetitions, because the review draws our attention to the points where God has touched us in prayer. And so both review and repetition, in their own ways, serve the purpose of getting the most out of our prayer, and receiving the graces of God with the maximum attention and reverence.

A repetition is often of value even when we feel there cannot be any more to come out of a mystery. From one day to the next, from one prayer session to the next, a great deal can alter, and we can often be surprised at how fresh and different a repetition can be from the first time round.

As we saw in Chapter 6 (p. 116), the fifth and last contemplation of an Ignatian retreat-day – the "application of the senses" – is the climax of these repetitions on a single mystery, or on a pair of inter-related mysteries. First we pray on the mystery, then we make repetitions of aspects of that mystery that particularly speak to us, and finally we dwell quietly with the help of our inner senses on the "points where the soul was more deeply moved and spiritual relish was greater" (227).

The same tools of repetition can be used outside of retreat as well as in. In fact there may be even greater need outside of retreat to maintain a sense of continuity and growth by a linking of scripture material or themes, rather than taking every prayer period as an isolated event.

And of course no amount of repetitions will exhaust the total meaning of a mystery. Another person, or even the same person a year later, may receive quite different insights. That is part of the mysterious nature of the mysteries of God: they are inexhaustible.

Reviewing a longer stretch

When, with the help of the review, we are noticing what happens to us in prayer, we can begin to notice not just what happens in one session, but where we are on a broader sweep. There is a whole cycle of Christian response, and if we can relate where we are to the overall pattern, then we can appreciate all the better the workings of God, and plan our prayer accordingly.

Much devotional writing has traditionally spoken of the Purgative, Illuminative and Unitive Ways. These three stages, broadly understood, can be found in the cycle of the liturgical year and, on a smaller scale, in the cycle of a single liturgy. They form the archetypal pattern of Christian response.

During the course of the year, we go through periods of penance (Advent and Lent), periods of quiet steady growth (the "ordinary" Sundays of the year), and periods of special joy and celebration (Christmas and the Easter season).

Within the course of the mass, we go through a similar sequence of responses to God, from the penitential opening (the "I confess" and "Lord have mercy"), through a section of listening and reflecting on scripture (the Liturgy of the Word), to a climax of mutual giving and communion (the Liturgy of the Eucharist).

In terms of the Spiritual Exercises the three Ways correspond to what Ignatius calls the First Week (the Purgative Way), the Second Week (the Illuminative Way) (10), and the Third and Fourth Weeks together with the *Contemplatio ad Amorem* (the Unitive Way).

The First Week exercises (which follow straight after the First Principle and Foundation) are concerned with sin and repentance. The Second Week exercises follow through the mysteries of the life of Christ, both in the infancy narratives and in the adult ministry. These are done in a spirit of identification with Jesus (the Kingdom exercise, which introduces the Second

Week, sets this theme). At the end of the Second Week we re-order our life in the light of this imitation of Christ (the Election). We are then ready to live through the passion with him (the Third Week), followed by the resurrection (the Fourth Week). Finally we contemplate God in a mutual exchange of love (the *Contemplatio ad Amorem*, see the final chapter).

None of these "Weeks" are actual weeks of seven days; in fact they will not be even in a month's retreat, for the Second Week is longer and more leisurely, and the length of each Week, together with the number and type of exercises per day, should be determined according to the needs of the individual retreatant. This is insisted on by Ignatius time and time again (17, 71, 129, 133, 162, 205, 209).

So repeatedly is the point made about adaptability, that it should be one of the chief watchwords of Ignatian method. It is regrettable that this basic principle of individual flexibility has so often been ignored in Ignatian retreats in the past (see p. 11).

And so, in the Spiritual Exercises, we can recognize the same cycle of purification (or purgation), getting to know Christ better (illumination), and being united in love with him (union). The Exercises correspond to the fundamental pattern of Christian response to God.

The consequence of this is that a retreat-giver can often notice retreatants passing automatically from one stage to the next of the Exercises, even before they have been told to move on. They will in the natural course of events become aware of their sinfulness soon after they begin the retreat; they will need to deal with it, through penitence, before they are able to proceed; they will slowly identify more and more with the call of Christ exemplified in the mysteries of his life; they will feel drawn to stay at his side in his passion, and to rejoice in sharing his resurrection. They will be filled with an increasing and overflowing love of God, that brings the retreat into their everyday life afterwards.

Even though the authentic Spiritual Exercises cannot be made without a director, he or she should not impose a shape on the retreatant's prayer, but rather observe and shed light on what is already going on. The task of the retreat-giver is to notice what is happening, and help the retreatant to notice too. The retreatant should not be moved on until she is ready, in terms of having found the fruit of that Week for herself.

It may happen that in the First Week some are slower in attaining what is sought, namely, contrition, sorrow, and tears for sin. Some, too, may be more diligent than others, and some more disturbed and tried by different spirits. It may be necessary, therefore, at times to shorten the Week, and at others to lengthen it. So in our search for the fruit that is proper to the matter assigned, we may have to do the same in all the subsequent Weeks. However, the Exercises should be finished in approximately thirty days. (4)

This principle of noticing how someone is progressing in the Exercises, and adapting the plan of the retreat according to where they are, is the exact parallel, on a longer time scale, of the review of prayer. After every prayer period we make a review, to notice what has happened in the last hour; after a day's prayer we see the director, to notice what has happened in the last twenty-four hours (in a 19th annotation retreat this will be more like once a week); and over the course of several days (or weeks) we notice the shape of the retreat, and move on to the next stage when the fruit of the present stage has been achieved – when we have found what we desire.

Outside of retreat the same process happens on a still longer scale. Many people see a spiritual director for what is known as on-going direction, and this may be once a month, or once a quarter, or whenever seems appropriate.

Those who do not have a spiritual director may observe the

same principle of noticing what is happening through other means – through a confessor, through discussions with a friend, through group sharing, through a spiritual journal, or just through the practice of occasional self-examination.

The longer the time scale, the more clearly we can see the direction we are moving in. The longer the time scale, the more amazed we are at the fidelity and creativity of God, who never lets us go but can turn every setback to advantage. "God works with those who love him . . . and turns everything to their good" (Romans 8:28). And St Augustine adds, "even my sins".

8

Being Sorry

Imagine Christ our Lord present before you upon the cross, and begin to speak with him, asking how it is that though he is the Creator, he has stooped to become human, and to pass from eternal life to death here in time, that thus he might die for our sins.

I shall also reflect upon myself and ask:
"What have I done for Christ?"
"What am I doing for Christ?"
"What ought I to do for Christ?"

As I behold Christ in this plight, nailed to the cross, I shall ponder upon what presents itself to my mind. (53)

Prayer is phony if sooner or later it does not lead us into being sorry for our sins.

Prayer is not just a soothing technique for self-improvement, and we do not pray to make ourselves feel good. A prayer life is not one of the luxuries of an over-fed, over-educated, over-developed western world – a final sign of physical, intellectual and spiritual well-being. It is about something much more probing and painful than that.

We pray because God made us, and we know that we must come up against that ultimate reality and acknowledge it is there. And that means knowing that God is great and good and that we are small and sinful.

Sorrow for sin, or contrition, is part of the natural cycle of response to God. We looked in the last chapter at the need to be sensitive to our inner resonances and the movements of the

Spirit within us. One of the feelings that we need to recognize, and that we will then be able to notice recurring every so often, is this sense of my sinfulness.

It may come about because of something I have done or because of an insight into the kind of person I am. Or it may not be as precise as that, but begin more as a feeling of discomfort that is not easy to locate. If I become aware of this unease, I may be able to recognize it as an existential sense that in some deep way part of me stands in the way of the free fulfilment of God's will.

This sense of sinfulness may emerge cyclically, so that about once or twice a year, perhaps, or more often, I find myself drawn to examine my conscience and spend a little time being aware that I am a sinner and asking for forgiveness. The less frequently I do this, the longer I will need to spend on it.

I may want to pray on my knees and hide my face in my hands. I may want to make an act of self-denial as a freely chosen sign that I am guilty. (We call that "doing penance".) I may want to tell my fellow-Christians that I have a dark side to my nature that they may be unaware of. I may want to make resolutions about re-ordering my life so that I will not make the same mistakes again.

What turns a purely human, earthly-bound sense of sinfulness and shame into a religious disposition of contrition, is the confident belief that God still loves me and wants to forgive me, and that the Church is there to mediate this forgiveness. My sins are not too much for God. Jesus died to free me from my sins, and he did not suffer a defeat but won a victory. So we do not despair or let ourselves be overcome by depression, but trustingly and humbly bring ourselves to be forgiven. Admitting my fault and asking forgiveness is a mature act. It is painful but creative and liberating.

There is always opportunity for making a public statement of my sinfulness in the liturgy. All eucharistic services, at least, begin with a public confession of sin and a reminder of God's forgiveness. Some of these general confessions are beautiful and touch deep parts of us that need to be brought before God. Here is an Anglican prayer of confession from the Alternative Service Book:

Almighty God, our heavenly Father,
We have sinned against you and against our neighbours,
in thought and word and deed,
through negligence, through weakness,
through our own deliberate fault.
We are truly sorry
and repent of all our sins.
For the sake of your Son Jesus Christ, who died for us,
forgive us all that is past;
and grant that we may serve you in newness of life
to the glory of your name. Amen.

Sometimes it is not enough to join in a community prayer like that. I want to do more, to dwell longer on my sins, to be more specific. It can be a cop-out if I never confess my sin in other than general terms, for I may become inured to the power of the formula, so that it ceases to challenge me.

Sometimes I need to say not just that we all have sinned, but that I in particular have sinned. And I need to say not just in general that I am a sinner but that I have done, or said, or thought, particular things of which I am now ashamed. I will feel a hypocrite if I do not confess them to a representative of my fellow-Christians and ask their forgiveness and prayers.

The sacrament of reconciliation, commonly known as confession, is a way in which some churches, notably the Catholic and Orthodox churches, meet this need. This sacrament is a great source of grace, for in it I meet Christ in an especially close way and hear his promise of forgiveness given personally to me for my own personal sins and shortcomings. No matter what I have done, even if I am a multiple murderer, all I need to do to gain the forgiveness of God and the Church is admit my sins and to be sorry for them. I am even promised a seal of confidentiality so sacred that not even to save his life or the lives of others may the priest break it.

This sacrament is not a burden demanded by the Church, but a privilege granted. It is not an empty ritual to be taken lightly and rushed through, but a profound act of prayer that reaches to the most vulnerable parts of the soul. To make the best use of the opportunity we need to prepare ourselves carefully beforehand, and enjoy our new-found closeness to God in prayer and thanksgiving after.

Ignatius emphasizes the importance of sacramental confession, and of a good preparation for it in examination of conscience (18, 354). In time of retreat, a general confession can sometimes be helpful, that is, a confession of one's whole life (44).

If we belong to a church that offers satisfactory conditions for receiving the sacrament it is good at least to consider making a confession once a year – ideally in the season before Easter when we are recalling Christ's passion. Praying over the passion should always have an element of contrition, as we are moved to feel "sorrow, compassion, and shame because the Lord is going to his suffering for my sins" (193).

Penance

When we want to make a gesture of our sorrow for what we have done or for the kind of people that we are, we can do penance. Penance is one kind of gift that we can offer to God, and we choose to do penance freely, because we want to make a gift. It is not a punishment that God inflicts on us.

We all have a desire to give as well as receive, so penance

corresponds to a deep human need. It should not be a burden, but a mercy, that the Church teaches that moderate acts of penance are pleasing to God.

The rule is, as always, to use penance in so far as it helps bring us closer to God. It may help as a token of sorrow for the past, or as an exercise in self-control, or as a way of begging God for something that I want, like the grace to be sorry or to know God's will for me (87).

It may be that I want to be sorry for my sins, but cannot find much response in myself. There is always an interplay between interior feelings and exterior actions, so just as we may make bodily gestures of prayer to rouse internal responses of reverence (see p. 25), so too we can make bodily acts of penance to rouse internal feelings of repentance. For this reason it may be more suitable to do penance before making a confession, while I am still seeking a true gift of contrition, rather than after, when any penance I am given by the priest will be nominal, and the more important emphasis is on thanksgiving for the grace God has given me.

Self-hatred is not a good reason, and has nothing to do with authentic penance. Feelings of self-hatred are more likely to lead to immoderate, undisciplined acts against our body, like excessive drinking or eating, or neurotic self-starvation as opposed to planned fasting.

Any self-sacrifice can count as a penance. It might be abstention from television watching, or walking instead of going by car, or making a financial donation to the poor, or giving up half-an-hour of my time to visit an old lady. But the three traditional areas of penance mentioned by Ignatius concern deprivation of food, or of sleep, or giving ourselves bodily pains (83–5).

Fasting has enjoyed a great come-back in recent years. We can cut out a meal or fast for a whole day. People who are experienced often fast for longer. We must never cut out water, as that would be dangerous to health. It is good if we can link our fasting to our sinfulness, by giving the money saved to an agency for relieving world hunger.

There are many other forms of penance regarding food that stop short of fasting. It has been traditional in some circles for children to give up sweets in Lent, and adults to give up sugar in tea and coffee. Some Catholics give up meat on Fridays – the day of Christ's passion – and many people have now given up meat altogether. It is very suitable to mark every Friday by some small act of penance, to remind us of Good Friday, just as we celebrate every Sunday to remind us of Easter Sunday.

There are endless variations along the same lines: margarine instead of butter, tomato soup instead of lobster soup, fruit or cheese instead of sweet or pudding. It is better to make a little sacrifice than none. But we should not become preoccupied with rules about eating: the control we exercise over our eating is only a tool to help us, not an end in itself. There is a real danger of eating rules becoming so important to us that they become distracting preoccupations instead of drawing our attention to God.

Abstention from alcohol is another good form of penance (211), whether just for one meal or for a week or a month or a year, depending on what would help each individual.

If we want to do penance in regard to our sleeping, we can sleep on the floor instead of in bed, or cut down our hours of sleep if they are more than we need. We have become so used to the soft comforts of modern civilized life, that it is good to remind ourselves from time to time that much of what we take for granted is really luxury. Plenty of people in the world sleep in hammocks or on the ground and do not come to any harm. But again it is important to stress that it is wrong to do any penance that damages the health.

Practices of beating the body with a discipline of knotted cords, or of wearing a hair-shirt or some other object that causes discomfort, are not currently fashionable. But despite a mood of suspicion and alarmist fears about masochism, there is no objection to their use if they are freely chosen for the right reasons, and if the pain they cause is superficial and does no actual damage (86). St Dominic used to beat himself heavily with chains, and Ignatius used to make holes in the soles of his shoes, as an act of penance.

Despite these paragraphs on physical penance, one of Ignatius' closest associates, John de Polanco tells us that "with regard to mortifications, I notice that he has a decided preference for those which attack one's love of honour and self-esteem rather than those which afflict the flesh" (Letter to Urban Fernandes, 1st June 1551). What I have said may serve to explain a little one of the sections of the *Spiritual Exercises* that people find most difficult today, but we should realize that, even in Ignatius' own estimations, physical penance is very unimportant. If it arouses the heart then it has achieved its purpose:

> The sacrifice acceptable to God is a broken spirit;
> a broken and contrite heart, O God, thou wilt not despise.
> (Psalm 51:17)

Examination of conscience: evil in the world

There are different ways of examining our conscience. The first approach is to begin from the evil of the world, to gain a sense of proportion and reality. Ignatius begins his section on sin in the Spiritual Exercises with considering sin first of all as something seen outside of myself that causes immense damage – the sin of the world (45–54). From a starting point of what really revolts us as evil we have a measure for recognizing similar roots of sinfulness as they are reflected in our own inner attitudes and temptations.

We all have feelings of guilt, and in our times of repentance we allow ourselves to recognize them and give them expression. But it is also important to educate our consciences. It can happen that we attach our guilt to the wrong matters – to minor sins that dominate our consciousness and prevent us seeing the real evil in the world. You could call it a deceit of the devil, if you go in for that kind of language, because it is one way in which something good starts in us which gets deflected so it ends up as something less good or even harmful (333).

Sin is blindness. That means that one of its effects is that we cannot see what our sins are. We know we are sinners, but we have to work at examining our consciences. We have also to pray for the grace to know our sins, if we are not to end up as blind as we began.

> For Isaiah again said,
> "He has blinded their eyes and hardened their heart,
> lest they should see with their eyes and perceive with their heart,
> and turn for me to heal them." (John 12: 39–40)

We spend so much of our lives in self-justification – "I did not do it", "I could not help it" – that we have to make something of an about-turn if we want to be open to seeing our sins. That is why the prayer to know our sins is important. It is another form of the prayer for what I want that we looked at on pp. 74–9. Do we really want to know what our sins are, or do we not dare? Sometimes it feels right to pray for as much knowledge of our sins as God knows that we are able to cope with at present.

To understand the seriousness of sin we have to look at what most revolts us as utterly evil. There are plenty of examples in the modern world – more, probably, than ever before: concentration camps, genocide, mass starvation, napalm, torture chambers, and the threat of nuclear devastation . . . If sin is about anything, it is about these. When we make the colloquy before the cross, given at the head of this chapter, we are looking at an archetypal example of that kind of sin – the violent destruction of the innocent.

If we allow our personal examination of conscience to be limited to the odd failure to say our night prayers, the rare oath uttered in a lazy moment, the occasional ripple of excitement in a private sexual act, we are blinding ourselves to the real nature of sin. The real evil is what leads people to do or collude in acts of abomination, and the real repentance is to recognize the roots of those sins in ourselves. One anonymous woman put it like this in a radio interview about her prayer:

> About five years ago I was reading a book about the war and someone who was in a concentration camp, and there was a part in it that was so horrible that I would not have been able to read it if I had known it was coming, and I was absolutely shaken by the cruelty of it. The awful thing was that I put the book down and I knew for the first time how it could have happened, and I thought, "It could have been me, committing those atrocities", and I don't think I've ever been so shaken or shocked or horrified in my life, and I've never been able to pray in the same way since. I can only pray now in penitence and in adoration because God is so tremendous when you set him against what you are.

The awful realization about our sinfulness is when we realize we could have been involved in acts that fill us with horror; or when we realize we are already implicated in evil situations that we collude in and do not speak out against, like the murder of the third world by the first world, or the preparations for nuclear war. The evil we can cause is far and away greater than anything we consciously intend. Our sin is to be blind to what we are doing, to let ourselves be swept along by

everyone else, so that we do not recognize our individual responsibility to dissent from communal acts of evil.

Too much attention on minor nit-picking makes me the
centre of the universe, whereas in fact a large part of sin is
getting myself out of proportion, as though I was more important
than anyone else. So even repentance can get distorted into a
disguised form of self-centredness, in which tiny personal sins
monopolize my horizon and obscure the broader issues.

Ignatius suggests we need to cut ourselves down to size in
various ways – first by seeing what evil means in terms of the
real world, in ways such as I have suggested.

Secondly, I can get a sense of proportion by seeing myself
as one of millions and millions of people – a short life in a
multitude of short lives; a corruptible body that will return to
dust and ashes (58). "Remember, man/woman, you are dust,
and to dust you will return", as we are told in the liturgy for
Ash Wednesday, as we receive the ashes on our forehead.
The Buddhist meditation on the corpse (see p. 110) is a good
one to use here.

Thirdly, I need to see myself and my sins in comparison
with God, who is at the same time infinitely great, and yet
intimately concerned in caring for me and preserving me,
despite my sinfulness (59). It is God's love that rescues me
from utter insignificance and gives me the dignity of being a
loved child of God.

Unless I have a sense of God's loving forgiveness, I am
unlikely to get far in my examination of conscience and
repentance, for I will be too scared to recognize my sins. Once
the weight of fear is lifted, once I begin to trust in the
unchanging nature of God's love for me, once I begin to taste
the lightness of being freed from my sins . . . then I find it less
difficult to admit how imperfect I am and how much hurt I
have caused or could cause.

Repentance can go wrong is if I am so weighed down by my

sins that I do not believe they can be fully forgiven. That can itself be a sin, for it is lack of trust in God. Another mistake is to try so hard to convince myself I am a sinner that I do not acknowledge the good that God has done in me, so that I put on a show of regarding myself as wholly evil. That is a lack of gratitude and recognition of God's work.

True repentance, by contrast, should lead me to feel closer to God, not intolerably cut off. Ignatius speaks of it as

> a cry of wonder accompanied by surging emotion as I pass in review all creatures. How is it that they have permitted me to live, and have sustained me in life! Why have the angels, though they are the sword of God's justice, tolerated me, guarded me, and prayed for me! Why have the saints interceded for me and asked favours for me! And the heavens, sun, moon, stars, and the elements; the fruits, birds, fishes, and other animals – why have they all been at my service! . . . (60)

In the light of all the opportunities and advantages that I have been given, I can see sin as an offence of ingratitude towards God. Sin is what makes me say, "I want more, and more, and more". It would not matter how much I am given, there never comes the point at which I say, "Ah, now I have my just deserts. From now on I am prepared to say thank you."

Sin is what prevents us seeing how much we have been given. Sin is what makes us forget about God. Sin is what keeps the door of our soul closed to Christ, so that we do not hear his knocking: "Behold, I stand at the door and knock" (Revelation 3:20). Sin is unresponsiveness, unawareness, insensitivity – what the scriptures call "hardness of heart", like the attitude of Othello as he planned to murder his wife:

Ay, let her rot, and perish, and be damned tonight; for she
shall not live. No, my heart is turned to stone; I strike it, and
it hurts my hand.

(Shakespeare, *Othello*, 4.1.189ff)

When Othello realizes what he has done after the murder, his
hardness turns to such sensitivity that he cannot bear to be alive
any more and to be confronted with the memory:

Whip me, ye devils,
From the possession of this heavenly sight!
Blow me about in winds! roast me in sulphur!
Wash me in steep-down gulfs of liquid fire! (5.2.276ff)

Our task in looking at our sins, is to have a realistic sensitivity to
their gravity without losing the trust that God can forgive them.
Despite the damage we have done, God can make all things well
and bring salvation.

"Shame and confusion" are truly part of penitence (48); so is
"a growing and intense sorrow and tears" (55) so is "a feeling of
abhorrence" (63). But, confronted by the mercy of God, I am
not destroyed by a realization of my sins. On the contrary,
because I am still loved I find I am able to stand before God,
more alive and healthy than ever,

extolling the mercy of God our Lord, pouring out my
thoughts to him, and giving thanks to him that up to this very
moment he has granted me life. (61)

It is this acceptance of forgiveness that gives me the strength to
reform myself and be confident that, with God's grace, I can live
a different life for the future. There is no sincere repentance
without an intention to change.

Examination of conscience: scripture

Another starting point for self-examination, that is indispensable for the Christian, is to use scripture.

The New Rite of Penance in the Catholic Church tries to recover a place for scripture in examination of conscience, by introducing a Liturgy of the Word into confession, just as there is a Liturgy of the Word in the mass. The idea is for priest and penitent to read together a passage of scripture, so that the confession of sins can be made in the context of the Word of God. In practice, this part of the rite is usually omitted (except in public liturgies of reconciliation), which makes it all the more important for the individual to use scripture in preparing for the sacrament.

If we are not examining our conscience in the light of the values of the Gospel, there is little point in being Christian. Even the Ten Commandments do not provide a sufficient guide, taken alone, to what God calls us to in the following of Christ, being based as they are on laws and transgressions. Jesus came to uncover the hidden heart of Old Testament morality, in the two great commandments "Love God", and "Love your neighbour as yourself" (Matthew 22:37–40). Any rules are only attempts to illustrate how we could make steps towards putting those great commandments into practice.

We all fall short of the standards offered us by Jesus. His sermon on the mount, for example, offers a high ideal for us to begin to work towards, in verses such as

"If any one forces you to go one mile, go with him two miles," (Matthew 5:41).

and

"You, therefore, must be perfect, as your heavenly Father is perfect" (Matthew 5:48).

Using a gospel passage for examination of conscience will remind us that we are not looking for transgressions so much as for partial failures to live out a challenging ideal of love. Jesus' parables on the forgiveness of sins are excellent texts to use; for example, the Pharisee and the Publican (Luke 18:9–14), the lost sheep (Luke 15:3–7), the lost coin (Luke 15:8–10).

One of the richest is the Prodigal Son (Luke 15:11–32). It shows how God waits for us to return, rushing out to meet us, putting a ring on our finger and feasting our return. It shows how sin can be the kind of rash foolishness that makes a mess of our lives, but also the mean goody-goody resentment about the fortune of others, illustrated by the elder son, with whom no one likes identifying. I can ask myself, "What is the pig-sty in my life?" I can also ask, "What is the fatted calf that I want to keep for myself?"

It is not just the moral teaching of Jesus that can be used for examination of conscience, but any mystery from his life. For example, if I pray over the entry into Jerusalem, I might become aware of how difficult I would find it to herald Jesus with that kind of abandoned celebration: I might become conscious that I am too reserved, or too fearful, or too sceptical to let myself give way to such jubilant praise of Christ.

Or I might be struck by Jesus' courage in entering the city where he knew he was to face death. I might wonder when I had shown courage in my life, and whether I would have been brave enough to follow him in those last days of crisis.

I might think about the fickleness of the crowd, who one day were meeting Jesus with cries of welcome and so soon afterwards were to cry out "Crucify him!" Do I show the same tendency to "go with the crowd" rather than act out of personal conviction?

Or again, it might be the aspect of the poor king, riding on a colt, that draws my attention: I might contrast my tendency to look up to the rich and powerful with the Christian invitation to find Jesus among the poor and simple. Whatever way the text challenges me I am unlikely to find myself as the spontaneously perfect disciple, unless I am cheating.

The passion always contains a particular invitation to repentance, because Jesus suffers to redeem us from our sins. But the same method can be used with any incident from the life of Christ. Just being with him is enough to point up some of my own deficiencies.

Examination of conscience: check-lists

It can also be very helpful to work through a check-list of one sort or another. Sometimes this can help us to notice faults that we would not otherwise think of. A list acts as a kind of external check, making sure we are not hedged in by our own prejudices and preoccupations.

Everyone has their own form of blindness. Some of the questions for self-examination that appear in the back of prayer books can strike us as having sexist assumptions or a lack of concern about social justice. So it can be helpful to make up our own list for examination of conscience as well as measuring ourselves against the questions of others. Our own list can also focus on what we know are our personal weaknesses and our personal vocation from God. An examination that does that is called a "particular examen", and when done frequently this can be a way of taking ourselves seriously in hand (24–31).

There are many different ways of dividing up sin. There are sins against God, sins against our neighbour, and sins against ourselves. There are sins of thought, word and deed. There are sins of action and omission. There are individual sins and communal sins, and so on.

The check-lists Ignatius suggests are the ten commandments, the seven capital sins, the three powers of the soul and the five senses of the body. He gives these in his First Method of Prayer (238–48).

The seven capital sins are pride, covetousness, lust, anger, gluttony, envy and sloth. That may sound rather melodramatic, largely because the words themselves are a bit archaic, but we can turn them into questions that make sense to us, and that may draw our attention to forgotten areas.

What am I proud about?

What are my ambitions

What does sex mean for me?

Have I shown anger and if so was it constructive? Have I suppressed anger in any areas of my life, and if so is it doing damage?

What am I dependent on in food and drink?

Have I got professional jealousies, or jealousies in relationships?

What am I lazy about?

We gain another dimension if, as Ignatius suggests, we turn our minds to the corresponding positive qualities. For example:

What is the gift of humility?

What would it be like to be less concerned with better status and possessions?

What would it mean to have a sexual drive directed towards the real purpose of sex?

What is the virtue of gentleness?

What is best for my health in eating and drinking?

What would it be like to desire the well-being and success of others without any envy?

For what causes would it be good to be able to work tirelessly? And so on

The three powers of the soul are memory, understanding and will. It is amazing what can be thrown up if we think about sin in these areas.

A sin of memory could be to pay too little attention to the moments of special joy and insight that I have been given. Remembering what led me to marry can refocus me on loving my partner. Remembering the joy of a conversion experience can make me realize how much I take God for granted. We can also sin in our memory by editing out the human misery that passes on the edge of our lives – the photos of starving children in charity advertisements; the threats to world peace that I prefer not to think about; the letter I should have written long ago to someone who is longing to hear from me.

We can sin in our understanding by having closed and prejudiced minds. What we allow ourselves to understand is largely governed by what we allow ourselves to see. We can convince ourselves of a whole range of opinions that are sinful because we ought to have known better – from "black people are better off under apartheid", to "infidelity to my wife does no harm so long as she does not find out".

We sin in our will when we fail to do the things we know we ought to do and mean to do but have never got round to doing. We sin in our will when we let ourselves drift through life following our inclinations, instead of deciding what would be good and taking more responsibility for decision-making.

Sinning with our five senses is either a matter of insensitivity and unresponsiveness, or of self-indulgence. Do I only look up to the sky to see whether to take an umbrella? Or do I live in constant appreciation of the stunning skyscapes that God provides for me every day? When I touch others am I saying "I care for you"? And so on.

In the same spirit as these suggestions of Ignatius, we could use as check-lists the beatitudes (Matthew 5:3–12) and the fruits of the Holy Spirit (Galatians 5:22–3). For example,

What would it mean for me to be poor in spirit?
Am I gentle?
Do I let myself mourn?
Do I hunger and thirst for justice?
To whom have I been merciful?
Is my heart set on the pure, single-minded search for God?
How can I be a peacemaker?
What could it mean for me to be persecuted in the cause of right?

Does my life show the fruits of love? joy? peace? patience? kindness? goodness? faithfulness? gentleness? self-control? In which do I most fall short?

There is one last approach to examination of conscience, that is so typically Ignatian and so richly revealing, that it is given in the appendix which now follows, as a self-contained exercise. It is called the general examen, and it is this type of examination that is most similar in approach to the review of prayer described in the preceding chapter. Unlike the other methods of examination of conscience, the general examen is something for every day, not necessarily as a formal, daily exercise, but at least as an informal, background reflection that fosters self-awareness.

Some forms of General Examen

Short Form

This can be practised at any time during the day but is especially suitable as a final thought in bed before falling asleep. It takes hardly any time so it can be done several times in one day. Although it is a short form, it incorporates the principles of the examen into a regular, instinctive habit of self-awareness.

Of the things that I have done today;

a) which do I now feel most happy about? I will thank God for these times.
b) which do I now feel most discomfort about? I will ask for God's help to cope better with such situations in the future, and, where fitting, I will say that I am sorry.

Longer Form

This is a rephrasing and expansion of Ignatius' general examen (43), that appears (with acknowledgements to J. Roger Greenwood) in John A. Veltri's Orientations *Vol. 1 (Loyola House, Guelph, Canada, 1979). It is called the "examen of consciousness". "Conscience" and "consciousness" are represented by the same word in Latin, and many people find this title more suitable and accurate. The examen follows Ignatius' five points: 1. give thanks; 2. ask for grace; 3. recall; 4. ask pardon; 5. resolve to amend. This exercise takes about a quarter of an hour. It is a good form of prayer to use in the evening, when it is natural for us to remember our day and look ahead to the next morning.*

Examen of consciousness

(This short prayer exercise is to help increase one's sensitivity to God working in one's life and to provide one with the enlightenment needed to co-operate and respond to his presence.)

Thanksgiving
Begin by looking over the day and asking to see where you need to be thankful. Do not choose what *you* think you should be thankful for; rather, by merely looking over the day, see what emerges, what you notice, even slightly. How do you feel towards what is shown to you? Do you see the giftedness of your life? Do you sense your own poverty? Allow gratitude to take hold of you and express this to the Father, Son and Spirit.

Ask for Light
This is a prayer for enlightenment from God not from your own analysis of the day. Therefore ask the Holy Spirit to show you what he wants you to see.

Finding God in All Things

Again look over the events of the day. This time ask the Lord to show you where he has been present in your life, either in you or in others, and what he has been asking of you. Look over your interior moods, feelings, urges, and movements, and see what stands out even slightly. Look for such things as joy, pain, turmoil, increase of love, anger, harmony, anxiety, freedom, enchainment, presence of God, isolation. In what general direction do you think you are *being drawn* by the Lord? How have you been *responding* to these experiences or situations that draw you towards the Lord and invite you to be more like Him?

More *particularly*, what attitudes are manifest in these experiences? Remember that your experience helps you to discover the underlying attitude, and your actions and choices flow from these attitudes. Is there any one place in your heart or any one attitude that the Lord is calling for conversion? Is there any one area you are being asked to focus your attention on, to pray more seriously over, to take action on? This is where your energy needs focus instead of on the many other things *you* think are important.

The Gifts of Sorrow, Forgiveness, and Gratitude

Seek forgiveness from the Lord for the moments you did not respond to his love. Do not be afraid to ask for the gift of an ever-deepening sorrow for not co-operating with him who loves you. Praise the Lord for those moments you have been co-operating with him.

Help and Guidance for Tomorrow

Ask the Father for your needs for tomorrow. For example, you may need to pray to overcome something – or to accept your "thorn in the flesh" – to persevere – to be more sensitive to the Lord's activity in your life – to let go – to love more – to have a conversion in some area – etc. There is *nothing* that can be done without God's loving assistance and guidance, so *ask*, *look for*, *trust* and co-operate with the Father, Son and Spirit living within you.

Examen of a Whole Life

Here is an example of how one could make an examen of one's entire life. It is best made with pen and paper to hand. The basic principles of the examen can be applied to any period of time – the preceding hour (as in the review of prayer), day, term, year . . . the time one has lived in the same place or done the same job . . . or one's entire life up till now.

1. I begin from the desire to see my life as part of salvation history. As well as the external human history, there is another dimension – the story of God's work in me. On the one hand are the opportunities God has provided; on the other are my half-hearted responses.

So I begin with thanking God for bringing me to where I now am.

2. I want this examination to be as honest as possible. So I ask God for knowledge of the truth, including knowledge of my sins.

3. This third point is the main part of the exercise. I make a note of the most important steps in my growing relationship with God (about eight is a good number). These steps, or stepping stones, may be single events, or they may be periods of growth. They may be explicitly religious, or they may be connected to the human process of maturing that I did not think of in terms of God at the time. I make a brief note of each as it occurs to me. Afterwards I can order them chronologically, so I have an idea of the overall shape of my life. There may also be steps backward, or anyway sideways.

When I have done this I am in a position to see what in my life I want to thank God for. I take time over this, being grateful for all that now seems positive in my history.

Only after I have done that do I look at the ways in which I have fallen short. Remembering the events that I am now grateful for, how could I have given more room in my life for the things that really matter?

4. I express my sorrow for the ways in which I have sinned and the areas of my life in which there is still an element of sin.

5. What priorities would I like to re-affirm for the future? Are there any practical steps I can take that would help re-direct my life on better lines?

I may close the exercise with an *Our Father*, which puts my request for forgiveness in the context of God's will for the world.

9

Loving Jesus

*Whenever the praise and glory of the Divine Majesty would be
equally served, in order to imitate and be in reality more like
Christ our Lord, I desire and choose poverty with Christ poor,
rather than riches; insults with Christ loaded with them, rather
than honours; I desire to be accounted as worthless and a fool for
Christ, rather than to be esteemed as wise and prudent in this
world. So Christ was treated before me. (167)*

We saw in Chapter 4 (pp. 74–7) how the grace we seek as we
pray over the life of Jesus, is to "know thee more clearly, love
thee more dearly, follow thee more nearly".

Many people who have made the Spiritual Exercises,
especially the Second Week, with its great emphasis on
following through the life and ministry of Christ, will say at the
end that what they have gained from the experience is a love of
Jesus. Even if they have tended to feel uncomfortable with that
type of language before – perhaps it seemed to them too easily
said, too soft and superficial – the long experience of the
Exercises will bring them to recognize that there is such a thing
as a personal relationship with Christ spoken of by
evangelicals. There is a real response of heart, mind and soul
that we make to Jesus that can only be called love.

This is of course by no means limited to the retreat
experience. We all have the responsibility to spend our lifetime
of Christian commitment dwelling on the mysteries of Jesus'
life – not only what he taught but even more what he did.

By living through Jesus' life with him we become more
conformed to his image. We join in the imitation or following of

Christ, not so much by looking inside ourselves and analysing what we are like (though that has a place, as we saw in the last chapter) as by looking outside ourselves at him, until we find that to keep our gaze on him we have to get up and move from where we are. We have to walk with him to stay in his presence.

And so both the preliminary prayer for grace and the concluding colloquy, in the classic Ignatian structure, concern themselves with this loving discipleship. First, in the prayer for grace,

> it will be to ask for an intimate knowledge of our Lord, who has become human for me, that I may love him more and follow him more closely. (104)

And finally, too, in the colloquy.

> according to the light that I have received, I will beg for grace to follow and imitate more closely our Lord, who has just become human for me. (109)

We can only dare make this journey of love with him because he first loved us, and came, like Hercules making his twelve labours, to win our love. He came

> that after many labours, after hunger, thirst, heat, and cold, after insults and outrages, he might die on the cross, and all this for me. (116)

That is why, in the colloquy before the cross that is given at the head of Chapter 8, I have my eyes firmly set on what he did for me before I ask myself what I should do for Christ.

Infancy

There are different stages in Jesus' life, and each stage has an invitation to me to follow.

One of the most human aspects of Christian tradition is the childhood of Christ. Though Jesus did not begin his active ministry until he was about thirty, Luke and Matthew's gospels give us precious stories from the infancy. This childhood sequence is the first stage of Jesus' life that Ignatius invites us to pray over.

There is the annunciation, when Mary received the news that she was to have a baby; the visitation, when Mary went to visit her cousin Elizabeth; the nativity, when Jesus was born; the visit of the shepherds and the wise men, when the Christ was recognized by those at the bottom of society and those at the top; the circumcision and presentation in the temple, when Jesus became part of the Jewish religious community; the flight into Egypt, when he became a refugee; the return from Egypt and the home-life at Nazareth, when he grew up in a carpenter's home, advancing in wisdom and grace; finally there is the losing and finding in the temple, when Mary was to learn how she could lose her son for three days as he went about his Father's business, and yet have him restored to her again.

Imagine how different our faith would be if there were no paintings of the Madonna and child, no celebrations of Jesus' birth, no tradition of the holy family. We would soon be in a religion for philosophers and intellectuals, instead of a faith for the poor, the illiterate, the young, the mentally handicapped, and for all people so that each one can find his or her own level of understanding.

Whether the historical details of these stories are accurate is of less importance than the fact that all the human life of Jesus, including his childhood, and babyhood, and life in the womb, are all affirmed as part of the way in which God took flesh for us.

Ministry

The second stage of Jesus' history is the most detailed, and this is the adult ministry, running from his journey to the River Jordan for baptism, up to his final entry into Jerusalem. These events form the largest part of the gospels, and we can gladly spend all our lives getting to know Jesus better from those accounts of his miracles and teaching, his journeying, his disputes with authority, his conversations with those who were searching, his making of the blind to see and the lame to walk. ·

There is a leisure to this exploration, because there is so much to see and to hear, even though the stories recorded in the Bible form only a tiny part of the whole history. "There are also many other things which Jesus did; were every one of them to be written, I suppose that the world itself could not contain the books that would be written" (John 21:25). We can allow ourselves to get to know Jesus gradually, over a long period of time, by following him around through these mysteries – perhaps first as a spectator, then as an actor in the scenes.

I said earlier (p. 139) that the cycle of Ignatian Exercises moves from the Purgative, through the Illuminative, to the Unitive Way. The Purgative Way clearly corresponds to what I was saying in the last chapter about "Being Sorry"; but the move from the Illuminative to the Unitive Ways is a gradual one. It has much to do with the way in which I am present to Christ in his mysteries. Illumination has more to do with finding out, with getting to know him; union has more to do with living in him and letting him live in me.

Anyone who receives the sacrament of the eucharist, even a child, shares in the Unitive Way by that action. I am part of the body of Christ, and the body of Christ becomes part of me. This indwelling is truly a mystery, which we try to understand better throughout our lives. It is an act that goes beyond any explanation.

Passion and resurrection

In the course of Jesus' life, by the time we reach the passion, the invitation is becoming increasingly clear. Do I just read about this as something that happened to someone else? Or do I want to go through the passion at his side? Do I say yes to it, accepting his death as a gift he makes to me, so that in some sense it becomes my death as well?

When I receive the body and blood of Christ in communion, that is what I am doing: saying yes to his death, as the path to salvation. I am in union with the Christ who suffered, died and rose again.

The passion, therefore, belongs very much to the Unitive Way. Only love can make sense of a choice like this – to be with Christ who suffers in his suffering – just as only love could make sense of God's own choice to become human so as to share in our suffering. Those who cry "masochism" have not understood the logic of love.

And so, in praying over the passion, Ignatius suggests that I

> ask for sorrow with Christ in sorrow, anguish with Christ in anguish, tears and deep grief because of the great affliction Christ endures for me. (203)

If I had not done that, what right would I have to make this prayer when I contemplate the resurrection? In this case I

> ask for the grace to be glad and rejoice intensely because of the great joy and the glory of Christ our Lord. (221)

It is joy not just at the salvation I receive, but the joy of seeing someone I love experiencing joy, so that I "feel joy and happiness at the great joy and happiness of Christ our Lord." (229)

Only love of Christ can make us want to suffer with him suffering and rejoice with him rejoicing.

The best parallel we know in human terms is the kind of love that leads to marriage. At an earlier point in the relationship we will keep company with someone because we love them and want to be with them. The love may grow to the point where all our desiring is drawn into wanting to be with them. We want to see them, listen to them, touch them.

But there is yet more: human love can reach the point when we want not only to be with them now, as they are today, but when we want to make an unconditional commitment to be with them all our life long. Even not knowing what the future will bring, or how the beloved will change and age, we want to tread the same path together. If they have cause for joy, we want to share it with them. If they suffer, we want to be at their side. We want to share their life with them more than we want to have the option of leaving the relationship if times become hard.

This is a high form of love, and human beings never live up to it fully all the time. In so far as we know that kind of love, we are really sharing in the love that God has for us. Enough people have glimpses of this kind of love for the following commitments to be made, under vow, in the sacrament of matrimony:

I, *N*, take you, *N*,
to be my wife/husband,
to have and to hold
from this day forward;
for better, for worse,
for richer, for poorer,
in sickness and in health,
to love and to cherish,
till death us do part,
according to God's holy law;
and this is my solemn vow.

The preferential option for the poor

When we have understood why people can take such extravagant vows as these, we are in a position to understand the passage quoted at the head of this chapter (from the Three Degrees of Humility, 165–7). It can sound so alarming and absurd at first, with its preference for poverty rather than riches, for insults rather than honours. Only love, with its determination to share all the life of the beloved, can make sense of this.

Christ could only accept death on a cross because he was motivated by love; and we can only make an option for poverty when we are motivated by love to be with Christ in his sisters and brothers who suffer.

The "preferential option for the poor" has now become one of the key ideas of the liberation theology that, spreading from Latin America, has captured the heart of Christians throughout the world. The particular formulation of the term is a new one, yet as early as Ignatius' Third Degree of Humility, we find the idea of such an option already expressed.

We can serve Christ in all people, not just in the poor; we can serve him in success as well as in failure; we can serve him when we have a position with status, and when we do not have status. Yet, where there is a choice, and where the work of God could be carried forward equally well either way, it is good to choose the lower path, because that is to imitate Jesus more closely.

It is an option we can exercise in every decision of life, when we choose a job or a home, when we choose food to eat or clothes to wear. This Third Degree of Humility is one step further than indifference, which is the Second Degree of Humility. Indifference says I am willing to accept either path, whichever God wills. The preferential option for the poor says that while I am willing to accept either path, I would prefer it to be the humbler one.

We see this option for the poor made by those who choose to be doctors in third-world situations of great hardship, when they could have had a comfortable practice in a western city; or by those who choose to be teachers in comprehensive schools in areas of urban deprivation, when they could have had jobs in smart schools of the private sector; or by those who choose to be missionaries in countries torn by civil war, when they could have served in a peaceful parish in rural England. There *are* people who so choose, and their motivation is love.

The Jesuit Refugee Service issued a statement on 21st November 1985 from Chiang Mai, Thailand, which included this passage, signed by all their regional co-ordinators:

> We try to place special emphasis on **being with** rather than **doing for**. We want our presence among refugees to be one of sharing with them, of accompaniment, of walking together along the same path. In so far as possible, we want to feel what they have felt, suffer as they have, share the same hopes and aspirations, see the world through their eyes. We ourselves would like to become one with the refugees and displaced people so that, all together, we can begin the search for a new life.

The accompaniment of the dispossessed, feeling what they have felt, is exactly what is meant by the preferential option for the poor, or the Third Degree of Humility.

Jesus said that those who would enter heaven would be the ones who gave him food when he was hungry, drink when he was thirsty, a welcome when he was a stranger, clothes when he was naked, and visited him when he was sick and in prison. And he said that as we did it to one of the least of his brothers or sisters, we did it to him (Matthew 25:40).

Christians who make the preferential option for the poor are those who do not just respond when they are confronted by the poor, the strangers, the sick and the imprisoned, but those who seek them out. They choose to go into the situations where they will meet people who are suffering, because they want to meet Christ. They act not out of duty or obedience, but out of their deepest desires, out of love of Christ.

Ignatius had a famous vision at a place called La Storta, just outside Rome, as he was on his way to seek recognition for his order from the Pope. He had an overwhelming sense of being told by God "I will be favourable to you in Rome" – even though, said Ignatius, he did not know what sort of outcome this would be: "I do not know what will happen to us in Rome, whether we will be crucified, or whatever else may happen. But I know this for certain: Jesus Christ will be favourable to us."

It seemed at the same time that he saw Christ with the cross on his shoulder, and next to him the Father, who said to Jesus of Ignatius: "I want you to take this man as your servant." Jesus took him and said, "I want you to serve us". It was as a result of this that Ignatius felt his brotherhood must be called the Society (or Company) of Jesus – those who keep company with Jesus, even as he goes to be crucified.

One of Ignatius' exercises that may be much influenced by this vision is called the Kingdom Exercise (91–8). Ignatius imagines an earthly king making an offer to his subjects to share in the same work, labouring side by side, by day and by night, on a basis of total equality (the same rations, the same clothes, etc.), with the promise that at the end they will share in the same rewards and victory. This is an analogy that is drawn from Ignatius' former life as a knight, and Ignatius is struck by the extraordinary generosity and humility a king would show were he to make an offer of such equality.

The next step is to apply this parable to Christ. Christ also says to each one of us:

> "It is my will to conquer the whole world and all my enemies, and thus to enter into the glory of my Father. Therefore, whoever wishes to join me in this enterprise must be willing to labour with me, that by following me in suffering, they may follow me in glory." (95)

The love shown by a God who offers such equal terms to human beings, draws out of Ignatius a generous response, in the words of the prayer "Eternal Lord of all things". It is a prayer that expresses again the desire for poverty with Christ poor, the desire that is known nowadays as "the preferential option for the poor".

- Eternal Lord of all things, in the presence of thy infinite goodness, and of thy glorious mother, and of all the saints of thy heavenly court, this is the offering of myself which I make with thy favour and help. I protest that it is my earnest desire and my deliberate choice, provided only it is for thy greater service and praise, to imitate thee in bearing all wrongs and all abuse and all poverty, both actual and spiritual, should thy most holy majesty deign to choose and admit me to such a state and way of life. (98)

The same idea, yet again, is expressed in another famous prayer traditionally ascribed to Ignatius, although probably much later in composition (see also p. 12). It was this prayer which we heard Father Gabriel, in *The Mission*, reciting when he accepted Rodrigo Mendoza into the Jesuits:

Lord, teach me to be generous.
Teach me to serve you as you deserve;
to give and not to count the cost,
to fight and not to heed the wounds,
to toil and not to seek for rest,
to labour and not to ask for any reward,
save that of knowing that I do your holy will.

It was certainly an option for the poor that led the Jesuits to go into the jungle and share the poor life of the Indians. Its eventual outcome was that they shared their death, which was also a sharing in the death of Jesus.

Those who, in love, die with him, will surely share in his resurrection. Those who, in love, desire to be placed with the Jesus who carries his cross, will surely find that the Lord will be favourable to them.

10

Discerning

Spiritual Consolation. *I call it consolation when an interior movement is aroused in the soul, by which it is inflamed with love of its Creator and Lord, and as a consequence, can love no creature on the face of the earth for its own sake, but only in the Creator of them all. It is likewise consolation when one sheds tears that move to the love of God, whether it be because of sorrow for sins, or because of the sufferings of Christ our Lord, or for any other reason that is immediately directed to the praise and service of God. Finally, I call consolation every increase of faith, hope, and love, and all interior joy that invites and attracts to what is heavenly and to the salvation of one's soul by filling it with peace and quiet in its Creator and Lord.*

Spiritual Desolation. *I call desolation what is entirely the opposite . . . as darkness of soul, turmoil of spirit, inclination to what is low and earthly, restlessness rising from many disturbances and temptations which lead to want of faith, want of hope, want of love. The soul is wholly slothful, tepid, sad, and separated, as it were, from its Creator and Lord. (316–7)*

Noticing the presence of consolation and desolation, and observing the way in which they work, is the basis of what is known as discernment.

We have all been given a sensitivity in our consciences to these different movements of the spirit, but we need to develop this sense and become practised in exercising it, very much in the ways described in Chapter 7, on *Noticing What Happens* (especially pp. 134–6), and in the General Examen exercises

177

given in the Appendix to Chapter 8. There we were already talking about discernment, about consolation and desolation, though without yet using those terms.

We can only discern for ourselves, not for others, for we do not have direct access to the inner experiences of another person. But by listening to what they tell us, and asking questions about their responses, we can draw attention to what is significant and help them make their own discernment. In that way we do not make their decisions for them, but help them to assemble data relevant to making their own decisions. This is always the task of an Ignatian spiritual director – not to tell you what to do, but to help you find out what to do for yourself.

How can the movements of consolation and desolation help us discern what is right? It is not, after all, a matter of just doing what I want, to secure the maximum happiness for myself. At least, it is not that on a superficial level. It is rather a matter of looking at the deepest possible level.

Ultimately, doing what God wants will make me happy and bring me the most profound and lasting peace. So in the end there should be no real conflict between what I want and what God wants, but in the short term there can be a lot of struggle about it. We need to be reassured that God wills our happiness, and does not systematically ask of us everything that we dislike doing.

When we discern we have to look honestly at what really brings us peace and gives us joy. We have to detach ourselves from our immediate desires and ask if these things that I desire really give me the satisfaction they promise. It is all like a blown-up case of sitting in front of a box of chocolates and having just one more, and just one more, and just one more, until I feel sick, and then looking in the mirror and seeing how fat and ugly I am, so then I have some more chocolates to cheer me up. It sounds stupid, but we all do that at one level or another.

Discernment means actually noticing that too many chocolates make me fat and make me feel sick, so that I can make a sensible decision about how many to eat. Thus consolation is not the briefly pleasurable feeling when I get my mouth on another chocolate. It is about the deeper and more long-lasting feelings of satisfaction.

Antoine de Saint-Exupéry expressed the same point this way. The little prince comes across a man who is drinking:

"Why are you drinking?", demanded the little prince.
"So that I may forget", replied the tippler.
"Forget what?", inquired the little prince, who already was sorry for him.
"Forget that I am ashamed", the tippler confessed, hanging his head.
"Ashamed of what?", insisted the little prince, who wanted to help him.
"Ashamed of my drinking!" The tippler brought his speech to an end, and shut himself up in an impregnable silence.
And the little prince went away, puzzled.
"The grown-ups are certainly very, very odd", he said to himself, as he continued on his journey. (*The Little Prince*, XII)

Here is how Ignatius learned this simple and obvious lesson for himself. When he was convalescing from his leg injury sustained in the siege of Pamplona, he had to stay in bed for months on end. He got very bored, and asked for some books to read. The books he liked were light, romantic fiction, but in the house where he was confined to bed they only had a life of Christ and some lives of the saints. He read them because there was nothing else.

When he was not reading he used to think for hours on end. Some of his thoughts came from his habitual, romantic imagination, but others were new fantasies inspired by the books he was reading – great deeds he would do, not this time for a noble lady, but for God, and this is what he noticed:

This succession of such diverse thoughts, either of the worldly deeds he wished to achieve or of the deeds of God that came to his imagination, lasted for a long time, and he always dwelt at length on the thought before him, until he tired of it and put it aside and turned to other matters.

Yet there was this difference. When he was thinking about the things of the world, he took much delight in them, but afterwards, when he was tired and put them aside, he found that he was dry and discontented. But when he thought of going to Jerusalem, barefoot and eating nothing but herbs and undergoing all the other rigours that he saw the saints had endured, not only was he consoled when he had these thoughts, but even after putting them aside, he remained content and happy. He did not wonder, however, at this; nor did he stop to ponder the difference until one time his eyes were opened a little, and he began to marvel at the difference and to reflect upon it, realizing from experience that some thoughts left him sad and others happy. Little by little he came to recognize the difference between the spirits that agitated him, one from the demon, the other from God.

(*The Autobiography of St Ignatius Loyola*, p. 24, trans. Joseph F. O'Callaghan, ed. by John C. Olin, Harper & Row, New York, 1974)

And so the Ignatian principle of discernment of spirits was born.

The difference between the more shallow feelings of attraction and a deep God-filled consolation is expressed by the American Jesuit John Carroll Futrell like this:

Confirmation that one has truly discerned and responded to the word of God often enough is a truly Paschal experience. This word often demands that a man conform more closely to Christ crucified and that his "yes" to God be the "yes" uttered by Jesus in Gethsemane, wrung from repugnance and fear and tears and blood, and leading to Calvary. Then, the confirmation is experienced – not at the top of the head, but at the bottom of the heart – in profound peace and in a power to act and to suffer with a joy that bears testimony that through this death the Spirit has brought about new life, the New Creation achieved in the Risen Christ. The "Amen" to the call of God is transformed by the Father in Christ through the Spirit into an "Alleluia".

(*Studies in the Spirituality of Jesuits*, April 1970, *Ignatian Discernment*, p. 64, American Assistancy Seminar on Jesuit Spirituality, St Louis, Missouri)

(More will be said on "confirmation" below, on p. 211.)

God does not give us misery – God gives joy and peace. And so Ignatius says in his Rules for the Discernment of Spirits (313–36) that in desolation "the evil spirit guides and counsels" (318). That does not necessarily mean we are in sin, but that we are in temptation. The good God does not tempt us, it is the devil who tempts us.

But the devil does not play a great role in the ordinary person's thinking nowadays, so there is little point in getting held up on questions of whether bad spirits exist or not. The point is simply to know that God brings happiness, and the times of sadness are when God has withdrawn a little to see how we get on when left more to our own devices. "Not very well", is the answer we have painfully to learn.

If it is not that God has withdrawn from us, but that we have withdrawn from God, then of course we will feel disturbance of soul. This can happen if, in a life basically turned towards God, we take a false track and do something that is wrong. It may be something that we know is wrong and that we have a bad conscience about. Or it may be that we are acting with sincerity but have been deceived. In that case the disquiet we feel may puzzle us and it may take a while to find out what is wrong.

But we can also feel disturbance of soul if we are leading a perfectly oblivious life of selfishness and self-indulgence, and then we get a twinge of anxiety that comes not from temptation this time, but from God. Ignatius says that in someone whose life is centred away from God, and whose fundamental option is against God, the action of the Holy Spirit will be to "rouse the sting of conscience and fill them with remorse" (314).

We saw earlier how Ignatius uses as an image of God's action "a drop of water penetrating a sponge", something that is "delicate, gentle, delightful" (335, see p. 136). The parallel effect of the bad spirit on someone seeking God is the opposite: it is "violent, noisy, and disturbing. It may be compared to a drop of water falling upon a stone" (335). But if we are turned basically away from God then our experience of the spirits is the other way round. Temptation feels easy and reassuring, and God's action, instead of being in harmony with the rest of our life, clashes disturbingly with it.

Another image that Ignatius uses is this: when our life is basically given to God, then the Holy Spirit can "enter silently, as one coming into his own house when the doors are open". We live in a basic state of peace, and the good things we choose are quietly in harmony with the whole. But if we are living a life of sin then the Holy Spirit can only "enter with noise and commotion that are easily perceived" (335). In other words, the feelings of great disturbance are caused by those movements that go against the fundamental direction of our life.

On the whole it is unlikely that anyone would be reading this book if they were intent on an evil and Godless life. But it is useful to make this point because it explains why some people can live in a very sinful way and never seem to notice anything is wrong. We cannot just say, "It must be all right if they do not feel a bad conscience about it". Ignatius explains why they do not feel a bad conscience – because even feeling a bad conscience shows that God must be in there working in some way, making them aware that something is wrong. And if they will not let God in at all then they can go on being irresponsibly selfish without being troubled by guilt.

Everyone will have their own examples of unrepentantly sinful behaviour of this sort. It could be a credit-card forger, who sees nothing more in life to look forward to than a round of night clubs, or a car thief whose only pleasure is in stealing the swishest cars and giving them a good run before smashing them up. It could be the sort of person who sends letters to sexual partners of the night before, saying "Congratulations, you have now joined the Aids club". It could be a Nazi officer, going home to enjoy a pleasurable family evening after consigning a few hundred Jews to the gas ovens. It could be a rich capitalist flopping lazily into a swimming pool in the South American heat, while thousands of peasants for whom he feels no responsibility starve outside his gate. Or it could be a leader of a drug-ring, feeling self-esteem because of his wealth, with no compassion for the lives he is ruining and the deaths he is causing.

All these people know they are doing wrong, but because they couldn't care less they put it from their minds and consolidate their position with more and more of the same behaviour.

Consolation and desolation

We can understand consolation and desolation more deeply if we look at the way these movements of the spirits operate when we pray.

One of the most comforting aspects of Ignatius' teaching – paradoxically – is his recognition that desolation is a regular part of our spiritual life. If one thinks prayer should always bring one peace and happiness as an immediate fruit one can feel doubly discouraged when it does not. Not only is there the desolation, but there is also the sense of inadequacy because one feels it is one's own fault for not praying properly.

Not so, according to Ignatius. Desolation is one of the regular things that happens when we pray. We can even expect it, from time to time. Our spiritual life goes in waves: with ups and downs. A down is not necessarily a sign that something is wrong. It may on the contrary be a sign of progress, in that it means we have progressed beyond our last pleasant plateau of consolation.

And so, when we are in desolation we should comfort ourselves with the knowledge "that consolation will soon return" (321). Equally, when we are in consolation we should not allow ourselves to become smug, for we know that there will be a "time of ensuing desolation", and we need to "store up a supply of strength as defence against that day" (323). Someone in consolation is urged "to recall how little we are able to do in time of desolation, when we are left without such grace or consolation" (324). And again, in desolation it is a comfort to know that such feelings of utter helplessness and weakness are not just mine but are a universal experience; they even point to the truth about our human condition.

When we are in consolation prayer is easy (13), and our commitment to God seems very rewarding. There is a whole range of feelings in consolation, from quiet calm to joyful ecstasy. But always in consolation we feel the lines of communication to God are open. Even if we are weeping – according to Ignatius tears of sorrow for sin can be one form of consolation – we feel the pain is a God-filled one. In consolation we feel that God is close.

In desolation, on the other hand, it is hard to pray. The time seems long (13) and God feels distant. We all know what it is like to be depressed. Desolation is a kind of depression, seen from the particular point of view of our relationship with God.

Nobody likes going through desolation, and although we know

it is quite normal and healthy to go through times of depression or desolation, it is also advisable to see whether there is any obvious cause that can be eliminated.

Ignatius says there are three principal reasons for desolation (322). Only the first of these is our fault: we may have neglected our spiritual life, so that it is not surprising that God feels distant. If we do not bother to pray it will not be surprising if we have little to sustain us spiritually.

The second reason is that the desolation may be a test. If we give to God when the giving is burdensome, how much more of a gift is that than to give when the giving is easy! Sticking out a time of prayer when it is hard is obviously far more virtuous than happily drifting through when prayer comes easily. Remaining faithful to our commitments – to God or to other people – when life feels against us is more of a pledge of love than doing the same when there is no sacrifice involved. And so although desolation is hard, it may be the privileged time for making progress.

The third reason is as a reminder that consolation is a gift, not something we can conjure up by our own efforts. Despite frequently mouthing beliefs about the importance of grace, we all have a terrible tendency to feel that prayer is something that we have achieved. We feel proud of our religious sentiments and imagine ourselves skilfully scaling a ladder to heaven, leaving many others far behind. When we start feeling like that it is time for God to withdraw the sense of facility, and give us a good dose of desolation to humble us, for

> God does not wish us . . . to rise up in spirit in a certain pride and vainglory and attribute to ourselves the devotion and other effects of spiritual consolation. (322)

It is reassuring to think of the great Christians who went through terrible periods of desolation, so that even when they were very close to God they could feel themselves a million miles away. Mary Ward (mentioned above on p. 36), at her time of greatest testing, felt like this:

> A fearful state of desolation was spread over her soul and all its powers. Filled with apprehension, she believed herself abandoned and forsaken by God, and beyond this, that she was even in a state of possession by the devil . . . and it was only by doing violence to herself that she continued her practice of daily communion.
>
> (*The Life of Mary Ward*, Mary Chambers, Vol. 2, p. 320, Burns and Oates, London, 1885)

Gerard Manley Hopkins wrote a series of poems at the end of his life called "the terrible sonnets". They include lines like this:

> No worst, there is none. Pitched past pitch of grief,
> More pangs will, schooled at forepangs, wilder wring.

and

> Wert thou my enemy, O thou my friend,
> How wouldst thou worse, I wonder, than thou dost
> Defeat, thwart me?

And yet Hopkins' dying words were to be, "I am so happy, so happy". He was not as far away from God as he felt, and when consolation returned to him on his deathbed, he was able to feel more happiness in God than if he had not suffered so much before.

One of the phrases that we associate with times of desolation is St John of the Cross's term "the dark night of the soul". Ignatius has no rigid theory of a succession of stages in the spiritual life, like a ladder to perfection. Probably the highly structured schemes of the Carmelites Teresa of Avila and John of the Cross recall their own spiritual journeys, rather than providing a blueprint to which every pilgrim is supposed to conform.

Ignatius' scheme is a looser: there are times of consolation; and there are times of desolation; and both belong to the pilgrimage. Even the sequence of purgative way, illuminative way and unitive way (see p. 139) is an ongoing cycle, not something that you get to the end of.

But Teresa and John of the Cross touch a deep chord in us when they write about prayer, even if we are not exactly sure which stage we are at or which mansion we are in. When we hear the phrase "the dark night of the soul" something in us resonates strongly, even if we do not know if our experiences have been the authentic "dark night" that he is speaking of.

We understand him to be saying something, in an elusive and poetical way, about the bad times not being all negative, just as the night is not all useless. The night is the condition for the dawn, and the dawn always comes. For a while we cannot see, we are cold, time drags, and we feel afraid. But we look ahead with hope:

> I wait for the Lord, my soul waits, and in his word I hope;
> my soul waits for the Lord
>   more than watchers for the morning. (Psalm 130)

In desolation we always have enough grace to remain faithful to God – "sufficient grace for eternal salvation" (320) – however hard it may feel, but what we do not have are the extra graces that make that service a joy. We will feel "agitations and temptations", but "the help of God . . . always remains, though we may not clearly perceive it" (320). We can be reassured that God will never allow us to be lost for lack of strength.

We are not totally helpless in times of desolation, for we can work against the temptation to give up by sticking to a discipline of prayer, as a firm framework to support us (13). The more we seek God's help, by prayer and even by penance (see p. 147), the more we learn the lesson of our total dependence on grace.

Because desolation is succeeded by consolation, it is important not to change our decisions when the times are bad. Even if a resolution or undertaking we have made does need to be altered, we will not see the situation clearly when we are feeling low. Ignatius says that when the evil spirit is guiding and counselling us "we can never find the way to a right decision" (318).

Everyone feels like throwing in their hand when they are in desolation, and these are the moments when virtues like fidelity and reliability are a great help. So it is better to keep to our commitments while we are on the downward wave, and when we have regained a measure of peace of mind we will be able to make a more objective, detached decision.

One example of this can be in retreat. When the retreat is going well, we have no difficulty in continuing. Then a bad patch can come, and we may feel like giving it up, feeling it is doing us no good. But if we can stick out the desolation we often come through to something good that we would never have found without that struggle. In times of desolation the retreat-giver needs to be very supportive, to help the retreatant to complete the undertaking made at the beginning. Otherwise a retreatant could become discouraged and half-hearted or even drop out just at the time when an important breakthrough could be made.

The same is true of work undertaken. If we have made a conscientious decision to do a job, and then later the difficulties make us feel like giving up, it is better to wait until we are over the hump before making a decision about staying or pulling out. We will be able to see the situation more objectively then. We cannot know if the difficulties are worth struggling through if we have not struggled through them.

This is not a recommendation for no change. There should be much re-evaluation, and great readiness to change our habits, our jobs and our lifestyle, but the times of trial are not the moments to make decisions on these matters. There is too much going on that could get in the way of a detached or "indifferent" state of mind (see pp. 38–43).

We all know people who cannot stick to their commitments, and who never get going on anything because they do not have perseverance. At the same time we also know people who can never bring themselves to change their commitments, however unhappy they are in them, because they lack courage. The balance needs to be somewhere between the two.

But it is not just a matter of finding a mid-point between perseverance and courage, for the right way is not always the moderate way – it may be an extreme way. It is more a matter of having the detachment and readiness to do God's will that will enable us to overcome our natural tendencies, whether they are to be unreliable or to be cowardly. With such detachment, or indifference, we will be better able to see what is right and to carry it out.

Decision-making on the basis of discerning our consolations and desolations will be discussed in greater detail in the next chapter.

Dryness

As well as desolation and consolation, there is another kind of experience known as dryness. This is when nothing seems to be happening at all. I pray, and feel neither satisfaction nor disturbance. I do not seem able to respond to God at all, even in a negative way.

Like desolation, dryness is one of the common experiences of prayer, that we have all known. It can be hard to go on praying when prayer is dry, not so much because we are distressed as because we are bored. Dryness often results in a form of desolation because we feel frustrated that our attempts to reach God seem to be blocked.

As with desolation, we should not be alarmed by dryness, for we know it happens to the best of us. But if the dryness continues we need to take a careful look at all the attendant circumstances.

On the whole, things should happen in prayer (6): they may be good things – consolation – or they may be agitations – desolation. The desolations do not have to be dramatic disturbances – just something going on. Similarly the consolations may be such gentle graces that we may not notice them until we become sensitive to the subtle movings of the Spirit. That is why it is so important to cultivate the art of noticing what is happening through the review, as was explained in Chapter 7. If we think absolutely nothing is happening we may be helped by a spiritual director to notice that more is going on than we had realized.

But there is a great deal we can do to help or hinder our prayer, and so, because of the rule "use what helps, avoid what hinders", dryness is always worth investigating (6). There is no point in making matters unnecessarily difficult for ourselves.

It may be that we are praying when we are tired, or in a noisy place, or making ourselves pray on our knees when we find that profoundly uncomfortable. It may be that we are taking too much material, so that we skate over the surface and nothing touches us: this is one of the most common causes of dryness. Sometimes it can be that we take too little material, so we have not enough to stimulate a response: if we clear our minds, wait for something to happen and nothing does, then it may be that we need to bring the scriptures into our prayer to feed it. It may be that we are not paying enough attention to preparation, so that we never give ourselves a chance to quieten down and open up to God. The review of prayer (see pp. 132–7) reminds us to check over questions of this sort.

Or it may be that God is trying to say something to us that we are resisting, and this can happen for a number of reasons, some of them in no way due to poor intention. This is when we can talk of hitting a block in prayer. We may have been praying quite fruitfully up till now, and suddenly we feel we cannot get through any more. If we can recognize that there actually is a block, that is the first step towards discovering what the block is.

For example, there may be something from my life that needs to be brought into my prayer. One woman found that prayer had been dry in the days following the birth of a nephew. She was thrilled by the child; and she had held him in her arms shortly after the birth. She had no children of her own, and now she was an aunt for the first time. Meanwhile nothing was happening in her prayer. Did she bring this baby into her prayer? No, she never thought of doing that, for she tried to clear her consciousness of all distractions, and have an empty mind.

It was not surprising she was hitting a block. Here was a life event crying out to be brought into the relationship with God, so important to her that it should have been the focus of her prayer. To block that off from her prayer was to block off the way God was trying to communicate with her.

Another way in which we can fail to hear what God is trying to say is when we over-programme what we think our responses should be. Another woman, praying on the passion, felt nothing, because she was trying to feel desolation. Her retreat came to a dead end – nothing was getting through at all – until she discovered that the gift God was trying to give her in the passion was not desolation but consolation. There was a joy of abandonment calling her, that she did not hear for fear of being happy while Jesus was being crucified. When she discovered that consolation as well as desolation can be a fitting response to Christ's passion, the block was overcome and the prayer flowed.

Another example is when we have an attachment that we do not want to give up. We want the prayer to be on our terms, and so we never let ourselves go in God's hands. Only if we can allow ourselves to bring all our life before God can the prayer really be free.

There can be many kinds of attachment that block our prayer – an area of sin from our past that we are frightened to look at; a clinging to wealth that we could not bear to lose; a comfortable life-style that we do not want to have questioned; a love affair that we fear is wrong but are not prepared to reconsider; a drug or drink dependence; a bitterness felt towards someone whom we do not want to forgive. When the problem is an attachment, we need to pray for indifference (see pp. 38–43). We can begin quite simply by acknowledging the problem and asking for God's help. Then, slowly, and probably over a period of time, we can relax our grip on our attachment, and feel how good the freedom is.

Distractions

One of the most frequent ways in which little patches of dryness creep into our prayer is in what are known as distractions. Everyone has distractions. It simply means that while we are trying to pray we find other thoughts coming instead.

There are distractions and distractions. Sometimes distractions just mean that we have not yet attempted to concentrate. We may have done little to still ourselves and enter into the presence of God, in the way spoken of on pp. 66–8, so that if we now turn our attention to praying the distraction goes.

Or it may be that there is something working away in the subconscious that needs a quiet time to float up to the surface. One mathematician used to find that the solution to equations she was struggling over would regularly come when she stopped to pray. Very sensibly she made the minimum fuss over this – she simply wrote down the answer and could then continue with her prayer undistracted by the fear of forgetting again.

If we can quietly turn our mind away from the distraction and get on with what we are choosing to do, that is, pray, then all is well. We want to forget the distraction so the less attention we pay to wandering thoughts, treating them as a problem, the better.

But there are also thoughts that people think of as distractions when they may in fact be the way in which God is suggesting a connection between prayer and life. If meditating on a passage from scripture leads us to think about a situation from everyday living, a memory from the past, or a hope for the future, then we could be resisting the action of the Spirit if we tried to shut it out again. The apparent distraction could be the very thing God is putting into our minds to pray over.

Sometimes the distraction is an anxiety that we live with and that troubles us so much that we cannot simply lay it aside. In a quiet time such as a time of prayer it fills our mind. In that case – since we cannot pray without the thought – we will have to learn to pray with it. We may bring it to the forefront and beg for God's help, like Jesus praying in the Garden of Gethsemane: "Father, if thou art willing, remove this cup from me; nevertheless not my will, but thine, be done." (Luke 22:42)

Or we may accept it as a constant theme, around which the rest of our prayer circles. This prayer or that prayer, this text or that text, this mystery or that mystery – all will be seen through the lens of the inescapable preoccupation. There can be value in this, even though we are struggling. The attempt to pray may soften our anxiety and make us a little more able to put all things into God's hands.

Deception

We can be tempted in two ways. We can be faced with something that we know perfectly well is against God's will: in that case we have a struggle between what we know is good, and evil. But we can also be tempted by evil masquerading as good: in that case we are not deliberately making a choice against

God but we may all the same be doing something very wrong and damaging.

It is this second sort of sin that afflicts religious people the most. They may lead what they believe are virtuous lives and yet be full of self-righteousness, intolerance, hypocrisy and self-importance. They know they are not the unrepentantly sinful types we looked at above (p. 183) – those who do not even attempt to do what is right. But in some ways this second type of sinner – the self-deceiving sinner – is a worse menace, because their sin is harder for them to recognize.

This was the sort of sin – the sin of the virtuous, religious people – that made Jesus angry. He always showed friendship and compassion to the straightforwardly "honest" sinners (like tax collectors or prostitutes – perhaps in our days we could say drug addicts or delinquents). They knew they were sinners so they were ready to hear the call to repentance. But the smarmy "holy" types drove him to distraction – the groups described as scribes and Pharisees, Sadducees and elders and chief priests.

"Beware of the leaven of the Pharisees and Sadducees", he says (Matthew 16:6). "The tax collectors and the harlots go into the kingdom of God before you" (Matthew 21:31). "Woe to you, scribes and Pharisees, hypocrites! for you are like whitewashed tombs, which outwardly appear beautiful, but within they are full of dead men's bones and all uncleanness. So you also outwardly appear righteous to people, but within you are full of hypocrisy and iniquity" (Matthew 23:27–8).

We have to beware of this kind of temptation, because the kind of people who go in for reading religious books are the ones who are liable to be tempted in this deceptive way, by evil disguising itself as good. We are not all as bad as the scribes and Pharisees, but our temptations are likely to go in that direction.

Ignatius explains the way this temptation operates in what are known as the Second Week Rules for the Discernment of Spirits (328–36).

When the one who is giving the Exercises perceives that the exercitant is being assailed and tempted under the appearance of good, then is the proper time to explain to them the rules of the Second Week. (10)

What tends to happen is that you start with something good, "holy and pious thoughts that are wholly in conformity with the sanctity of the soul" (332). For example, you might start with the desire to work for higher moral standards and for religious orthodoxy. These are good things; but they can sometimes result in a narrow and intolerant attitude that one then claims is the will of God. Or you might start with the desire for more freedom and greater openness to the modern world. These things too are good; but they can occasionally lead to a loss of faith and an undiscriminating acceptance of worldly values.

You can start with promoting peace and end up absolutizing your own political theories. You can start with supporting stable, firm government and end up putting all your critics in jail. You can start with seeing many ways in which the Church needs reform and end up forming a new sect of your own. There are endless ways in which something that begins well can become distorted and go astray.

So Ignatius warns:

We must carefully observe the whole course of our thoughts. If the beginning and middle and end of the course of thoughts are wholly good and directed to what is entirely right, it is a sign that they are from the good angel. But the course of thoughts suggested to us may terminate in something evil, or distracting, or less good than the soul had formerly proposed to do. Again, it may end in what weakens the soul, or disquiets it; or by destroying the peace, tranquillity, and quiet which it had before, it may cause disturbance to the soul. (333)

When this happens we are advised

> to review immediately the whole course of the temptation. Let us consider the series of good thoughts, how they arose, how the evil one gradually attempted to make us step down from the state of spiritual delight and joy in which we were, till finally he drew us to his wicked designs. (334)

Whether we call this the deceit of the devil or mere self-deception does not matter. In a way it is more compassionate to us to blame the deception on the devil, not on ourselves. But the point is simply that the deception does not come from the Holy Spirit, but from another source that diverts us from God. This kind of distortion is a standard part of our spiritual struggle, and we should not be ashamed to admit it happens to us. We need to be aware of the dangers and learn to unmask the falsehoods.

There can also be deception the other way round. We have been considering temptations that deceive us because they appear to begin as the work of God though they then go astray. But there can also be the temptation to drop a good plan because we have scruples about our motivation. Ignatius considers these in "Some Notes Concerning Scruples" (345–51).

For example, I may make a perfectly good decision to pray for a quarter of an hour every day during Lent. I have considered the matter and made a conscientious choice about it before God. But after a few days, when the chosen time of my prayer comes round, the thought slips into my head that my first duty is to be doing many needed tasks for my family. I think that the time of prayer – may be precisely because I want to do it – is perhaps a self-indulgence. So in my indecision I let the prayer drop, and in this way a good and God-inspired plan is spoiled.

Or I may have decided to do a sponsored walk for those hit

by an earthquake. After I have had the idea I begin to wonder if I am not doing it to draw attention to myself: I like the feeling of advertising my physical feats and appearing virtuously altruistic at the same time. So I wonder if the whole idea is not a disguised form of self-aggrandisement, and I give it up. But the earthquake victims then get no assistance, and I have no further plans to help them.

Ignatius has advice for these occasions, when a good plan is interfered with by the fear that it

> is motivated by vainglory or some other imperfect intention, etc. In such cases we should raise our mind to our Creator and Lord, and if we see that what we are about to do is in keeping with God's service, or at least not opposed to it, we should act directly against the temptation. According to St Bernard, we must answer the tempter, "I did not undertake this because of you, and I am not going to reliquish it because of you." (351)

Some people are far more prone to scruples like this than others. On the whole we may notice that those with a tendency to worry about their intentions like this can usually be recommended to set their hesitations aside and go ahead: the fact that they are having these worries at all is often a sign that the operative motivation is a good one. On the other hand, there are others who are not nearly sensitive enough to their own hidden agenda: they need to be encouraged to become more self-questioning and less certain of their own rightness.

It is valuable to become aware of which kind of person one is, so that one can adjust towards the other direction, rather than becoming more and more scrupulous on the one hand, or more and more thick-skinned on the other (349). A scheme that sometimes helps people to recognize their personality type in ways like this is the Jungian-based Myers-Briggs workshop, which can now be done at several retreat houses.

There is one more type of deception that needs to be spoken of. This can be quite dangerous, because one is so certain that one is inspired by God.

There is a kind of religious experience called by Ignatius "consolation without preceding cause" (330, 336). This may be the same as or similar to what Teresa of Avila called the "prayer of union", and John of the Cross called the "substantial touch of the Lord". Sometimes people call this a revelation, or a vision. Usually a discernment of God's will takes time, but when we have had a "consolation without preceding cause" then we *just know*.

When Ignatius says the consolation has had no preceding cause he means there is no explanation for what has happened – we have been suddenly flooded with a sense of God's presence, such that the experience could only have come directly from God. "God alone can give consolation to the soul without any previous cause" (330).

Usually God works in us through the normal laws of causality – for example, I feel uplifted at church because the service has been well planned, with good music, and everyone there feels uplifted, or because it centres around particular themes that are important to me at the time, etc.; I feel consolation in prayer because I am reaping the fruits of concentration, vulnerability, persistence, etc. But exceptionally we can feel consolation, at church, at prayer, on the train, or anywhere, when there is apparently no explanation for it. It is an unexpected grace, an unmistakable touch of God.

It is good that the Rules for the Discernment of Spirits recognize the existence and validity of these experiences: they are far less uncommon than we might think, though people tend to keep quiet about them in case they are thought to be nuts. But though Ignatius recognizes these experiences, he also draws attention to the way in which they can go wrong and deceive us, so that we think we are inspired by God when we are not.

When consolation is without previous cause, as was said, there can be no deception in it, since it can proceed from God our Lord only. But a spiritual person who has received such a consolation must consider it very attentively, and must cautiously distinguish the actual time of the consolation from the period which follows it. At such a time the soul is still fervent and favoured with the grace and after-effects of the consolation which has passed. In this second period the soul frequently forms various resolutions and plans which are not granted directly by God our Lord. They may come from our own reasoning on the relations of our concepts and on the consequences of our judgements, or they may come from the good or evil spirit. Hence, they must be carefully examined before they are given full approval and put into execution. (336)

An example of this could be the story of St Francis of Assisi, when he prayed before a crucifix that spoke to him. "Francis, go and rebuild my Church – it is falling down", said the crucified Christ. Francis collected stones and made a fine job of repairing the building. But something was wrong – somehow that was not the end of the matter. Francis had had a genuine vision, but he had not properly interpreted it. When he thought the job was done he had to go back and look at the pure essence of the revelation again. The rebuilding of the Church that Francis was called to was more than a matter of stones and mortar.

In a contemporary event like the claimed appearances of Mary at Medjugorje, this is the kind of analysis that helps. There may be an unmistakable touch of God about what is happening. But is the whole interpretation of the event correct from start to finish? That is another question, to which I do not know the answer. It is not a matter of accepting the whole Medjugorje phenomenon or rejecting it, as an all-or-nothing choice. God does not deceive, but there are so many ways in which we can misunderstand.

Again, it can happen that someone feels he or she has a vocation to the priesthood, when they do not. What may have happened is that they have felt a genuine call to devote their life and service to God, and have automatically assumed that that meant priestly ordination, without realizing there are other ways of being wholly given to the Christian ministry

Many people who think they are prophets, but who go astray and found new sects or new religions, are probably being misled in the same way. There may be a genuine religious experience at the start, but we cannot accept all that they think God is telling them.

It is not that God deceives, but that they have confused the essence of God's revelation to them with their own subsequent conclusions about it. The excitement and aura of the presence of God has seemed to bathe in the same light thoughts and resolutions that came afterwards and are no longer directly from God. And so we have to be cautious about the ways in which we articulate and interpret our experiences of God's call to us, and be ready to look for ways in which we have overlaid the purity of God's original word.

In the next chapter we will continue the study of discernment, looking at how to put the principles of discernment into practice in the making of decisions.

11

Decision-making

I must not subject and fit the end to the means, but the means to the end. Many first choose marriage, which is a means, and secondarily the service of God our Lord in marriage, though the service of God is the end. So also others first choose to have benefices, and afterwards to serve God in them. Such persons do not go directly to God, but want God to conform wholly to their inordinate attachments. Consequently, they make of the end a means, and of the means an end. As a result, what they ought to seek first, they seek last. (169)

What has decision-making to do with prayer? It has everything to do with prayer.

One of the greatest pitfalls for people who go in for spirituality, is to waft around in a spiritual zone seeking peace, fulfilment and inner harmony, and leaving the world to rot. Centres of spirituality flourish, master's degrees are taken in prayer, meditation becomes a boom industry, and meanwhile the hungry go on being hungry, the naked go on being naked, the sick and imprisoned have no one to visit them, and the sinful structures of the world continue unchallenged.

For someone in the third world, a spirituality movement can be bad news. The theologians of liberation draw attention to the implicitly conservative nature of most of these movements when they are found in Latin America – like the Cursillo retreat movement, and the Charismatic renewal: by turning attention away from the bitter reality of the way people live, they leave everything the way it was.

That is why Ignatius' insight is crucially important – and very modern. He insists that deep experience of prayer must be interlinked with very practical and concrete decisions about the way we live our life. "Love", he says, "ought to manifest itself in deeds rather than in words" (230).

We can recall again his summing up of the purpose of his Spiritual Exercises:

> Which have as their purpose the conquest of self and the regulation of one's life in such a way that no decision is made under the influence of any inordinate attachment. (21)

That is very oriented towards a practical outcome – regulating our lives so that we make decisions, and make them in indifference (see pp. 38–43).

But it is not all practical politics: before we make any conclusions about ordering our own life for the future, we are given a thorough drenching in the life of Christ. For those who are making the full Spiritual Exercises, long contemplations on the ministry of Jesus precede the Election material, when I consider what implications all this has on the way I lead my life.

Ignatius avoids in this way both a spirituality separated from action, and action that has no deep roots in spirituality. Contemplation and life are in dialogue; neither is allowed a free rein alone.

By "the regulation of one's life" Ignatius really does mean getting down to the nuts and bolts and not staying on an exalted, idealized plane. Those who are "really to attain this end", namely, the purpose of their creation, are going to "have to examine and weigh in all its details" their life-style (189). Two questions predominate in Ignatius' mind: responsibility for others and economics.

We are responsible not just for our families but, in different degrees, for many others besides. In Ignatius' day it was easier to see who you were responsible for – the servants of your household, for example, whom you had to organize efficiently and justly, educate, and guide by your example (189).

But in the modern world the situation is more complex for we have so many levels of responsibility. A great deal of thought and working out is required. We have more responsibility as franchised members of a democracy, than those who were under a monarchy. We have more responsibility living in the age of the media explosion than those who would not normally have the opportunity to communicate with those outside their immediate area. We have more responsibility as investors in a wide range of financial undertakings (through shares, insurance policies and so on) than those who could see with their own eyes how their money was used. We even have more responsibility in a Church that is in a state of ferment and is developing many new ministries than those who knew clearly the division between a priest's and a lay person's tasks.

There have always been the occasional saints like Ignatius or Catherine of Siena, like Francis of Assisi or Bridget of Sweden, who disrupted the normal sharing out of tasks by playing new roles and sticking their noses into others' affairs – aware that they had a responsibility to Church or state beyond what was apparent to the average eye. But they have been rarities. Today we can less easily escape the very wide-ranging responsibilities that fall on us all, particularly in the first world where we have so much power.

Ignatius gives us no answers, but he does give us the questions.

As for the economic decision-making, with Ignatius' questions of nitty-gritty practicality – this is possibly the area of his teaching most frequently slid over as not relevant to today. But it is more relevant than ever today, when the gap between rich and poor is so much greater.

Economically we have to make choices (and not just drift into them) about how large a house to have, whether to employ anybody – in the home or in business – and if so how many, what proportion of our income should be spent on family and home, and how much should be given to the poor or put to religious purposes (189). Rather terrifyingly, Ignatius calls to mind (in his Rules for the Distribution of Alms, 337–44) the example of Anna and Joachim (Jesus' grandparents) who, according to tradition, divided their resources into three parts:

> The first they gave to the poor. The second they donated to the ministrations and services of the Temple. The third they used for the support of themselves and their household. (344)

That goes quite a bit further than the ten per cent tithing familiar to the medieval Church, which in itself feels a big step for most Christians today. The richer we have become the less we give away.

He also tells us that "the Third Council of Carthage, at which St Augustine was present, decided and decreed that the furniture of the bishop should be cheap and poor" (344), and he suggests this has a lesson not only for bishops (some Latin American bishops live like this today) but also for those in all walks of life.

These are not models that we are urged to copy, but examples of how people have worked out the imitation of Christ for themselves. They give the right flavour of seriousness to the consideration. The task for each one of us is to make our own discernment on these matters, so as to seek the will of God for our own life.

"How can I know what is God's will for me?" is one of the most frequent questions asked by Christians who are sincerely exploring their faith. Some people work on the basis of rules: they know God's will from obedience to the ten commandments and the laws of the Church, for example, or to their superior, if they are in religious life. Rules of this sort are inevitably limited and approximate, and tend either to focus on what is forbidden more than on positive initiatives, or to be somewhat vague.

Obedience is important – it is a matter of belonging to one body, and there is a basic level of obedience that applies to all members of the Church and not just to those in religious orders. We cannot ignore the ten commandments, the rules of the Church or the instructions of religious superiors. Ignatius esteemed these highly, as is shown, for example, in his Rules for Thinking with the Church (352–70). At the same time we can note that these Rules are not concerned so much with what we should and should not do, as with what we should and should not value and praise: they are designed to foster the right "attitude of mind" (352) rather than to be a sufficient guide to behaviour.

When we have done all things in obedience we have still not even begun on the work of individual discernment. Discernment is a principle that can be applied to any situation, and that helps us to find the will of God for each one of us personally, in quite concrete ways. Ignatius' guidelines on discernment are far more flexible than any list of rules can ever be.

The last chapter was about noticing what are called the movements of the spirits – in other words, consolation and desolation – and observing how they relate to the guidance of the Holy Spirit. This chapter will focus in a practical way on the stages of a discernment process, when we consciously and systematically make use of this data to make a decision about what to do in our lives.

Discernment is something that we can learn to exercise in every decision of our lives. Some decisions are small and are not worth making a great fuss about, but we can always try to remain open to the slight movements of consolation and desolation, and the general examen (see Appendix to Chapter 8) is specifically designed to foster this awareness on an everyday level.

The discernment process

Let us suppose now that there is some major question we need to make a decision about. It may be whether to marry someone. It may be a choice of career. It may be whether to give up a job and strike out afresh. It may be whether to move house, or even whether to go and live in another country. It may be what sort of schooling to give my children. It is a sufficiently important question to be worth taking time over deciding, as the consequences one way or the other will be far-reaching. How do I make a "discerned" decision?

In the first place one realizes that "discernment" is not just a label one slaps onto any decision to hallow it. The heart of discernment is that it is made through prayer. I am not just asking "Do I want to do this?" but "Does God want me to do this?" We misuse the term if we call a purely reasoned, prudential decision a discernment.

There is nothing wrong with making decisions just on the basis of reasoning, so long as they are not major decisions: there is not time in life to go through a discernment process on everything. But if a systematic searching for God's will in prayer is not undertaken, it is not a discerned decision and should not be called such.

This point needs to be made because in some religious orders in some countries discernment has got itself a bad name, where a controversial decision has been taken – sometimes by higher authority and sometimes by democratic vote – and has been called a discerned decision, even though there has been no real discernment process. Calling it a discerned decision is a way of commending it, but the result has sometimes been that people feel that "if that is discernment, I want none of it", so there can be damage in using the term too loosely. It can be a shady way of claiming that God is on our side when we feel we need to lay claim to extra support.

At the same time, discernment does not bypass the normal investigative and reasoning processes, as though we had a hotline to God to which facts and information were irrelevant. Therefore, the first and essential step in a discernment is to find out all relevant data. It is irresponsible to make an important decision on a basis of inadequate knowledge. The facts will be the first part of our data, but they will not be our only data.

Next, because we are looking for the will of God, no matter what that is, we need to be as close as possible to a state of indifference. The importance of indifference for discerning a decision cannot be too strongly emphasized (169, 179). In other words, we need really to be prepared to go either way; we need to be in that state of balance or equilibrium in which we can face both alternatives. We need to pray for indifference as to the outcome, expressing our willingness to God to go one way, or the other.

> I should beg God our Lord to deign to move my will, and to bring to my mind what I ought to do in this matter that would be more for his praise and glory. (180)

In the quotation at the head of this chapter we can see what subtle ways people have of sliding past indifference. Almost everyone has been guilty of first deciding the basic shape of their lives – this marriage, that job – and then convincing themselves that serving God means inserting a bit of charity into what has been predecided. There are notable exceptions – people, for example, who in their growing conversion to God feel they want to change their way of life, take up a different career, and so on. But they are the minority.

Most religious schools send their pupils out with exactly the same values for life decisions as any unbeliever: a good job is one where there is little danger of unemployment and good prospects of pay and advancement. God is brought in to sanctify this process and inject some Christian principles into it *after* the main lines of the decision have already been made.

One woman who left her convent found how strong such assumptions were in family and friends. One moment she had been living a life of poverty, chastity and obedience. The next moment – because she was no longer in the "nun" category – she was expected to assume a totally different way of life and behave like a "proper" lay person, getting a reliable job and settling in to climb up the worldly ladder. But she did not want to drop every value she had tried to live by up till then.

She wanted to do work that God wanted, not work that the world expected. She distressed her relatives by working for no money in a self-help group for the unemployed, rather than getting herself a proper job that would be less worthwhile. She had tried to seek Christ first, and to use work as a way to Christ, but they wanted her to seek work first, and Christ as a way of sanctifying that work. People who attempt to go against the values of the world like this, and to take the Gospel at face value, have a hard time being understood.

So we need indifference if we are to be truly open to the will of God, not just on the edges of our life but in the radical heart of our basic life choices. We need to be able to face one way or the other, with the readiness to do what God wants, no matter what it is.

But while we must be prepared for either outcome it will not help to face both alternatives simultaneously. That would leave us not so much in balance, as sitting on the fence. To develop greater indifference we need not just to say to ourselves that we are seeking the will of God in general, but really to face each alternative wholeheartedly. We need not just to see the proposed course of action as a remote theoretical possibility, but really to put ourselves in the attitude of mind of going in that direction and making that decision. Then we will know that we are ready to do it for God, if that is right.

There is another reason for making a time lag between the two options. It is important to be able to observe the difference in our responses to each alternative, and for that we need a little space – a day, for example, or longer on a big decision, a week, a month, or more – to see how we feel about each. If we mentally move straight from one to the other and back again we will not get a very clear picture. Response to one alternative will get in the way of responses to the other, and neither will have the chance to form properly because we will not have entered fully into that state of mind.

Suppose I have reasonably adequate information about a proposed job, and I am ready to make a discernment. On day one of the discernment I will pray to know the will of God and to follow it. I will then propose to myself: "I shall take the job". I make, as fully as I am able, a commitment of my heart to this proposition, even though it is still only an experimental thought and I am not yet committing myself in reality. I offer this hypothetical decision to God in prayer.

I notice how I feel about it in prayer. I live with it through the succeeding day, letting my thoughts come back to it frequently. I observe what it does to me. For example, it may feel immediately right. I may feel consolation. Perhaps I feel a burst of unexpected lightness and confidence; or perhaps it is just a quiet sense of being in a pair of shoes that do not rub. On the other hand, I may feel desolation. The job may feel onerous, like a tedious and rather unnecessary encumberment. Or again, the responses may take a little time to settle down. I may feel initially scared, and afterwards a sense of freedom when I have really brought myself to face the possibility. Or I may feel initial enthusiasm, that progressively fades. Or I may feel nothing much at all. All of this I observe in myself.

On day two, in prayer, I offer God the other alternative: "I shall not take the job". I try to make this commitment as total as the other had been. Again I make myself live through the day in the spirit of this decision. I notice what that does to me.

Probably by the end of the second day I will know quite clearly which way is right, because that decision has felt right and the other one wrong. Not only will I have made the right decision, but I will *know* that I have made the right decision, which will give me great strength aginst temptations and second thoughts later on.

But sometimes the answer is not clear. It may be that I was not really indifferent, and that is clogging up my freedom to be receptive to the promptings of the Spirit. It may be that the decision needs a longer period of information-gathering. It may be that I need to live with each option for much longer than a day – a week, perhaps, or even several months.

It can also be that I have asked the question in the wrong way. For example, I may be thinking of taking the new job or staying with the present one, but perhaps neither job is right. For this reason it is best to formulate the question as *a or not-a*, rather than *a or b*. If *a* does not feel right I do not automatically leap to the conclusion *b*. I may have to do a discernment on *b or not-b*.

Ignatius describes how someone might make a discernment like this:

> We might offer to God one day to follow one path, another day another path. . . . Then we are to observe what preference God indicates as his will. This would be like offering various dishes to a prince to see which of them pleases him.
>
> (*Directory to the Exercises*, 1599, Chapter 27)

Suppose I think I have discerned the fruits of the Holy Spirit on one of my alternatives – peace or freedom or joy – so that I make my decision for that option. There now begins the final stage of the discernment process – that of confirmation. This is never finally concluded, but is always open to further confirmation. Like all the other stages in the discernment, it begins with prayer:

> After such a choice or decision, the one who has made it must turn with great diligence to prayer in the presence of God our Lord, and offer him the choice that the Divine Majesty may deign to accept and confirm it if it is for his greater service and praise. (183)

The confirmation will continue as the choice is lived out in life. Often we will just get on with life without constantly harking back to the question of whether we have chosen well, and that is good because it is a sign that our choice has been good. But if we notice unease and tension continuing, and perhaps increasing, over a period of time, we may need to go back to the choice from which it stems and reconsider whether we have not perhaps misinterpreted our discernment of spirits and taken a wrong turning.

Going through a discernment process to make a decision is not a guarantee that what we conclude is right really is right. There is no infallibility about discerning, and we should not be led into speaking as though we had God's will in our pocket, just because we have discerned and prayed: we can still make mistakes.

But what the discernment process does mean is that we will have conscientiously taken all possible steps towards recognizing God's will. We will have done the best that can be done to find out what is right and to make Mary's prayer our own: "I am the servant of the Lord. May it be done to me according to your word" (Luke 1:38).

Some exercises

There are some exercises given by Ignatius which are helpful in making decisions. One of the areas for which they are particularly recommended is in organizing our finances, so as to decide what proportion to give to charity (338–41). But they can also be used for any kind of decision (178–88).

We will not need to use exercises like this if we are already clear about what to do: they are not a necessary prerequisite for a discerned decision, but an aid to clarity when no clear answer has yet emerged.

For example, some decisions seem to be made not by us but by God. When St Paul heard his voice on the road to Damascus, he knew "without hesitation, or the possibility of hesitation" (175) what he had to do. It was the same when Jesus called his apostles to follow him. This is what Ignatius calls the First Time for making a decision. We considered experiences like this under the category of "consolation without preceding cause" in the last chapter (pp. 198–200). Going through a series of testing exercises would be absurd in a context like that.

It would also be unnecessary if we already know what to do, not this time with an unquestionable inner certainty, but when strong feelings of consolation and desolation make it clear enough what path we should take (176). Ignatius calls this the Second Time for making a decision. But if we do not yet have that kind of clarity about what to do, then we may be in the Third Time, which is "a time of tranquillity" (177), when one is feeling calm and collected and ready to make a rational and objective assessment. That is when these exercises may be helpful.

The exercises assume, as explained above, that we have decided on a clear question – "Should I do this or not?" (178), that we are seeking the will of God (179) and that the exercise takes place in the context of prayer (180).

The first exercise (what Ignatius calls the First Way, in the Third Time) is to make four lists. The first will be the advantages and benefits of doing whatever it is I am considering. The second will be the disadvantages and dangers of doing it. The third will be the advantages and benefits of not doing it. The fourth will be the disadvantages and dangers of not doing it.

I now have a fairly exhaustive list of pros and cons. But remember that all this is happening under the presupposition that I want to serve God. So factors like "will be good for my reputation" or "will give good pay" are not in themselves going to be very persuasive.

Having made this analytical examination of the questions I now make a decision based on reason. I let the stronger and better arguments prevail. Finally I offer the decision up to God in Prayer for confirmation.

The next three exercises are similar to each other, and can go together. (Together Ignatius calls them the Second Way, in the Third Time.)

First, I imagine someone I do not know in the same situation as I am in (185, 339). I see what advice I would want to give to him or her – still assuming of course, as always, that it is not their reputation or income one wants to promote but the kingdom of God. The effect of this is to distance myself a little from the question, to gain more objectivity.

Secondly, I imagine I am on my deathbed. What decision would I hope to have taken looking back from that perspective (186, 340)? Thirdly, I imagine my life is over and I am before Christ for his judgement. I want to stand before him without regret, so what decision would I wish to have made then (187, 341)? The effect of this is to abstract myself from the influence of short-term benefits and to bring my ultimate values to the foreground.

The motivation that should impel me in these exercises is the love of God. Love of neighbour, of course, is part of love of God: it is God who moves us to care for others (184, 338). Love moves us even though we will probably not be getting any nice warm, woozy feelings but will be operating on a more objective, rational plane. Ignatius is suspicious of decisions made in the fervour of the emotions, particularly if the person has an unstable temperament or if rational considerations make the choice look unrealistic (14). Love does not exclude being reasonable, on the contrary, it demands it.

And so even a bit of structured analysis like this is part of prayer. It is a way in which we focus on our love of God, and see where that love leads us.

Communal discernment

Supposing a decision is not just mine to make? Supposing it affects my family, or those I live with, or my colleagues at work, or the local Christian community? Given that discernment is no infallible answer, I cannot do my discernment exercises on their behalf, and then tell them what they are supposed to do.

There are, however, methods of community discernment that can be used very profitably if you are fortunate enough to have a community or colleagues or family who all accept the Ignatian method, or at least are willing to give it a try. Even in many Jesuit communities you can find reluctance to use the ways of communal discernment, but a rediscovery of this authentic tradition is growing. In a recent letter to the Society of Jesus, their General, Peter-Hans Kolvenbach, looks forward to more occasions of discernment in groups of Jesuits and laity working together (*On Apostolic Discernment in Common*, 5th November 1986, paragraphs 22, 33, 40).

In its simplest form the members of a group go off and pray individually, seeking God's guidance on the question in hand. Then they return and share their thoughts and insights and the way God moved them in prayer. This sharing is received with respect by the others, and a decision emerges. It is not a matter of winning points, knocking down arguments, and gaining a majority vote, but of being open to the promptings of the Spirit in one's own prayer and in the prayed-over reflections of others.

One way in which this is put into practice is in a Jesuit General Congregation, for the election of a new General. For four days the members of the congregation are together in a prayerful, retreat-like atmosphere. In this period they ask questions of each other to find out more about anyone they are considering voting for. But there is no meeting in groups, no campaigning, no plotting policies – just an exchange of information. At the end of the four days they gather as a Congregation, but before voting they pray over their decision in silence for an hour. Then they cast their votes.

With this method, Generals have been elected almost unanimously, when a few days earlier no one had any idea who the front-runners were, and even when there had seemed to be division over what sort of leadership was wanted anyway. Communal discernment is a method that helps to unite people, because it focuses them on their common desires in the sight of God rather than exacerbating the points of conflict. It turns what could be a sordid political manoeuvre into an experience of the power of the Holy Spirit.

One of the best examples of a communal discernment was the way in which Ignatius and the first companions decided whether or not to make a vow of obedience to one of their number: in other words it was this discernment that resulted in the formation of the Society of Jesus, in 1539.

The first question they put to themselves was whether or not to remain united in one body, rather than to disperse. This was easily agreed: they felt they could serve Christ more effectively if they stayed united, and they all experienced the fruits of the Spirit over that decision.

Next they had to decide what sort of body they should be,

and this focused down to the precise question of whether they should take a vow of obedience. (They had already taken vows of poverty and chastity at Montmarte in 1534.) It was much harder to arrive at a common mind on this point.

They prayed more persistently for guidance, and during the day they kept silence to allow greater space for the discernment of spirits in their personal prayer. Then on the evening of the first day, each one gave the reasons against vowing obedience, which he had found through his own prayer and reflection. After the next day's silent prayer, each gave his reasons in favour of it.

This separation of pros and cons is the same as the practice, in individual discernment, of committing oneself to one option on one day and the other one the next day. It helps clarity and indifference. But we can see why it might be especially valuable in communal discernment.

Most groups have some strong and vociferous personalities, capable of making the rest feel rather small and stupid if they disagree. If these people can be engaged to fight on both sides, first one and then the other, then we can really be assured that both cases will be well put. As Kolvenbach's letter points out, "the presence in a community of one eccentric, aggressive, or cynical personality is enough to call into question the possibility of discernment in common" (Paragraph 14.) By allowing pros only one evening, and cons only on another, you not only can neutralize such personality factors, but can even put them to good advantage – providing you can get people to follow the rules.

It is best to have someone in charge of organizing the way the discernment is done, so that it does not break up as people argue over how to proceed: this can be either a leader from within the group, or someone from outside who has no personal involvement in the question but facilitates the process.

Each group or family can adapt these principles of

communal discernment according to their situation, and according to the gravity of the decision in hand. The main things to remember are the importance of seeking God's will, and the value of being structured and disciplined in the operation – not just deciding in the way you would anyway, and then calling that "discernment", Finally, it is important to remember that the period of confirmation is just as relevant in a community decision as in an individual one: time will tell if all is well.

An example

Making discernment a habit of mind means living it out in our lives over a period of time, observing our own movements of consolation and desolation and how they relate to the decisions we make. We can learn the theory of discernment, but we will not have appropriated it and made it our own until we have become used to seeing how discernment works in the way we live our lives. In the meantime an example may help to give a sense of discernment as a real life experience.

The example comes from Thomas Merton's autobiography *The Seven Storey Mountain* – a book full of discernment data from beginning to end.

The first time he had the thought "I am going to be a priest" (while sitting on the floor playing records and eating breakfast) it came not as "a thing of passion or of fancy" but as "a strong and sweet and deep and insistent attraction . . . something in the order of conscience, a new and profound and clear sense that this was what I really ought to do" (p. 253, Sheldon Press, London, 1975).

But Merton was told, in a disastrously mis-handled confession, that someone like himself, with his past sins and present confusions (the past included an illegitimate child, though that did not become public knowledge until after his

217

death), "certainly did not belong in the monastery, still less the priesthood".

> When I came out of that ordeal, I was completely broken in pieces. I could not keep back the tears, which ran down between the fingers of the hands in which I concealed my face. So I prayed before the Tabernacle and the big stone crucified Christ above the altar.
>
> The only thing I knew, besides my own tremendous misery, was that I must no longer consider that I had a vocation to the cloister. (p. 298)

He commits himself to seeking God as a layman and gets a teaching job, but he keeps on having experiences that re-activate his desires. Looking through the *Catholic Encyclopedia* one day he is deeply disturbed by what he sees about Cistercians (Trappists) and other contemplatives:

> The thought of those monasteries, those remote choirs, those cells, those hermitages, those cloisters, those men in their cowls, the poor monks, the men who had become nothing, shattered my heart.
>
> In an instant the desire of those solitudes was wide open within me like a wound.
>
> I had to slam the book shut on the picture of Camaldoli and the bearded hermits standing in the stone street of cells, and I went out of the library, trying to stamp out the embers that had broken into flame, there, for an instant, within me.
>
> No, it was useless: I did not have a vocation, and I was not for the cloister, for the priesthood. Had I not been told that definitely enough? Did I have to have that beaten into my head all over again before I could believe it? (p. 318)

He continues to follow the path of a layman, and decides to go and live among the poor in Harlem. When he gives this news to his boss (whom he respects greatly) he is asked if he has ever thought of becoming a priest. He answers,

> "Oh, yes, I have thought about it, Father. But I don't believe I have that vocation."
>
> The words made me unhappy. But I forgot them immediately, when Father Thomas said, with a sigh:
>
> "All right, then. Go to Harlem if you must." (pp. 359–60)

But he is not able to escape the thought of priesthood.

> Finally, on the Thursday of that week, in the evening, I suddenly found myself filled with a vivid conviction:
>
> "The time has come for me to go and be a Trappist."
>
> Where had the thought come from? All I knew was that it was suddenly there. And it was something powerful, irresistible, clear.
>
> I picked up a little book called *The Cistercian Life*, which I had bought at Gethsemani, and turned over the pages, as if they had something more to tell me. They seemed to me to be all written in words of flame and fire. (p. 363)

In confusion and distress Merton goes outside to pray by a statue of St Teresa of Lisieux. He says, "You show me what to do."

> Suddenly, as soon as I had made that prayer, I became aware of the wood, the trees, the dark hills, the wet night wind, and then, clearer than any of these obvious realities, in my imagination, I started to hear the great bell of Gethsemani ringing in the night – the bell in the big grey tower, ringing and ringing, as if it were just behind the first hill. The impression made me breathless, and I had to think

twice to realize that it was only in my imagination that I was hearing the bell of the Trappist Abbey ringing in the dark. Yet, as I afterwards calculated, it was just about that time that the bell is rung every night for the *Salve Regina*, towards the end of Compline.

The bell seemed to be telling me where I belonged – as if it were calling me home. (pp. 364–5)

He goes straightaway to talk to a priest and ask his advice:

As soon as I proposed all my hesitations and questions to him, Father Philotheus said that he could see no reason why I shouldn't want to enter a monastery and become a priest.

It may seem irrational, but at that moment, it was if scales fell off my own eyes, and looking back on all my worries and questions, I could see clearly how empty and futile they had been. . . . But now everything was straight again. And already I was full of peace and assurance – the consciousness that everything was right, and that a straight road had opened out, clear and smooth, ahead of me. (p. 365)

It is some eighteen months since Merton was told he had no vocation for religious life. He becomes a Cistercian monk and remains one till his death at the age of fifty-three. Despite many frustrations and sometimes seemingly unnecessary limitations, he finds at Gethsemani a life in which he is able to serve the Church.

His books, including *The Seven Storey Mountain* and his works on prayer, such as *Seeds of Contemplation*, influence many people. He makes an important contribution to the inter-faith dialogue by his interest in eastern religions.

He helps to rediscover the hermit vocation within monasticism, and goes to live in a hermitage at a distance from the monastery. Later he seeks to move to a stricter order, the Camaldolese, and is refused permission.

There are temptations and difficulties, but his basic life-choice to be a monk seems to be confirmed, though at the same time the meaning of being a monk is much explored and many assumptions are tested and refined. Photos of Merton before his death show a jolly, laughing man, bubbling over with exuberance.

We can see from this example, how major decisions are inevitably guided by the principles of discernment, whether or not we use that terminology or know the theory. If it matters enough, God will get the message through to us in the end. With Merton, the movements of the Spirit had to become very dramatic indeed – he came close to a direct and unmistakable call from God – before he realized that his earlier, conscientious decision against the priesthood was mistaken.

But it does help enormously if we can consciously recognize the principles of discernment and the hand of God in our lives. It helps partly because it stops us wasting time trying to do the wrong thing and "kicking against the pricks", and partly because the constant presence of God's guidance in our daily lives is a source of joy and reason for regular thanksgiving.

12

Finding God in All Things

Take, Lord and receive all my liberty,
my memory, my understanding, and my entire will –
all that I have and call my own.
You have given it all to me.
To you, Lord, I return it.
Everything is yours; do with it what you will.
Give me only your love and your grace.
That is enough for me. (234)

At the very end of Ignatius' Spiritual Exercises he begins to talk about love. Love is not a word he uses lightly.

"Faith, hope, love abide, these three; but the greatest of these is love" (1 Corinthians 13:13). All the same, it is a word that is cheapened by over-use, and while we can easily see how true that is in human relationships, it can also be true of our relationship with God.

It is a powerful word, if we really know what it means. And so the last Exercise – when we dare to name what it is that draws us to God – is called the *Contemplatio ad Amorem*, literally, the Contemplation towards Love. Its full Latin title – rarely used – is the *Contemplatio ad Amorem Spiritualem in Nobis Excitandum*, literally the Contemplation to arouse spiritual love in us, and this is rendered in various ways, all a little clumsy: the Contemplation to Obtain Love; the Contemplation to Attain the Love of God; the Contemplation on the Love of God. But I prefer to keep the Latin, *Contemplatio as Amorem*, because in its brief simplicity it seems to cover both the idea that I am contemplating God's love for me, and the idea that I am making this contemplation in order to grow in love myself.

Prayer in the end is a matter of the heart rather than the head. We will use our heads, have thoughts, insights, ideas or whatever, but prayer begins to be effective when this work of the head reaches the heart.

Anthony de Mello says in *Sadhana*,

> The head is not a very good place for prayer. It is not a bad place for *starting* your prayer. But if your prayer stays there too long and doesn't move into the heart it will gradually dry up and prove tiresome and frustrating. You must learn to move out of the area of thinking and talking and move into the area of feeling, sensing, loving, intuiting. That is the area where contemplation is born and prayer becomes a transforming power and a source of never-ending delight and peace. (p. 13)

When prayer reaches the heart we feel our desires altered. We discover a love of God within us that we did not know was there. We give praise and rejoice because we feel praise and rejoicing. We want to be with God, to serve Christ, to live in the freedom of the Spirit. We understand what the Psalmist meant by verses like these – because we are beginning to feel something of the same ourselves:

> My soul is feasted as with marrow and fat,
> and my mouth praises thee with joyful lips,
> when I think of thee upon my bed,
> and meditate on thee in the watches of the night;
> for thou hast been my help,
> and in the shadow of thy wings I sing for joy. (Psalm 63:5–7)

Sometimes the word "affectivity" is used for this feeling-level of our response, as opposed to the more intellectual responses that come from our head. Here is a passage from the fourteenth-century English hermit, Richard Rolle, that is every bit as relevant today as when he wrote it:

> Nowadays too many are consumed with a desire for knowledge rather than for love, so that they scarcely know what love is or what is its delight. Yet all their study should have been directed to this end, so that they might be consumed with the love of God as well. Shame on them! An old woman can be more expert in the love of God – and less worldly too – than your theologian with his useless study. He does it for vanity, to get a reputation, to obtain stipends and official positions. Such a fellow ought to be entitled not "Doctor" but "Fool"! (*The Fire of Love*, Chapter 5)

That is a passage that may appeal to us greatly in our anti-intellectual moods, but of course the point is not to knock theology but to ask whether it is being used to bring us closer to God and awaken love in us. We are not talking about the superficial feelings but the deep orientations that determine our choices. "For where your treasure is, there will your heart be also" (Matthew 6:21).

Pascal said, "The heart has its reasons which are unknown to reason" (*Pensées*, 224). The Indian Jesuit Herbert Alphonso, currently director of the Centre for Ignatian Spirituality in Rome, used to say in his lectures, "No transformation takes place unless the truth reaches the heart. And the truth does not reach the heart except by slow assimilation."

The final contemplation

Many of the ideas of the *Contemplatio ad Amorem* appear in earlier writers, particularly in a twelfth-century monk, Aelred of Rievaulx, who had a similar triple meditation designed to awaken

and inflame in us the love of God. Aelred's text influenced
Ludolph of Saxony's *Life of Christ*, which Ignatius read in his
convalescence. But what is distinctive to Ignatius' Contemplation
is that while Aelred's great vision of God's love filling things and
sustaining creation is in terms of the world to come, Ignatius finds
that love already poured out in the world in which we live.
Ignatius' mysticism concentrates on the present moment: he finds
God in all things now.

There is no need to have gone through the sequence of the
Spiritual Exercises before making this Contemplation: it is so
much the key to Ignatius' entire approach to the spiritual life that
we can make this way of prayer our own at all times and in all
places.

In a way it is the First Principle and Foundation all over again –
that basic assumption about our purpose here on this earth (see
Chapters 1 and 2); but in the *Contemplatio* our relationship with
our creator is illumined by being seen in the terms of love. This
time it is not just the dry consideration that God is our end, and so
we ought to work towards that end in our lives: it is the awakening
of the deep desire to give ourselves to God in love, for God has so
loved us. What in the First Principle and Foundation might have
had a touch of duty about it, is now transformed by the intimate
knowledge of a God whom we have come to trust and with whom
we long to live for ever.

Ignatius begins the *Contemplatio ad Amorem* by making two
observations: first, "that love ought to manifest itself in deeds
rather than in words" (230). Secondly, "love consists in a mutual
sharing of goods" (231), and he uses the example of lovers. If we
are to understand what it means to love God we are going to need
to understand what it means to love another person:

> "The lover gives and shares with the beloved what he pos-
> sesses, or something of that which he has or is able to give; and
> vice versa, the beloved shares with the lover. Hence, if one has

knowledge, he or she shares it with the one who does not possess it; and so also if one has honours, or riches. Thus, one always gives to the other. (231)

"One always gives to the other", and in the exchange one does not lose but gain. Love shared is love increased, and gain comes not through accumulation but through continual interchange, so that one can never say, "Our love is great enough now, let us keep it where it is". We never tire of the cycle of giving and receiving, in which we do not just hand back as though rejecting the gift but we give ourselves back along with it.

> I will ponder with great affection how much God our Lord has done for me, and how much he has given me of what he possesses, and finally, how much, as far as he can, the same Lord desires to give himself to me according to his divine decrees.
>
> Then I will reflect upon myself, and consider, according to all reason and justice, what I ought to offer the Divine Majesty, that is, all I possess and myself with it. Thus, as one would do who is moved by great feeling, I will make this offering of myself. (234)

There then follows the prayer, *Take and receive*, which is printed at the head of this chapter. We can also use Julian of Norwich's prayer (see p. 48), in which she expresses the ideas of the *Take and receive* in her own words.

> God of your goodness give me yourself, for you are enough for me and I may ask nothing that is less, that may be full worship to you. And if I ask anything that is less, I am always wanting – but only in you I have all. (*Showings*, Chapter 5)

Or this phrase from Ignatius' great admirer, Mary Ward, puts it in a sentence:

I will give him what I have, and all I need I will find in him.

The *Take and receive* is such a generous prayer that it can terrify us or it can excite us; but what Ignatius is suggesting is that, even if we do not happen to feel the great waves of love that would make us long to abandon ourselves in this way to God, we can still recognize that it is good and right, so that we choose to make the offering. When we have chosen to act according to love, our love will grow.

God's presence is to be found in all things, in all that we see and do and experience. In the *Contemplatio ad Amorem* the world is no enemy, but rather the ongoing sign and expression of God's love.

God dwells in creatures: in the elements giving them existence, in the plants giving them life, in the animals conferring upon them sensation, in human beings bestowing understanding. So he dwells in me and gives me being, life, sensation, intelligence; and makes a temple of me, since I am created in the likeness and image of the Divine Majesty. (235)

It is not just that God created the world long ago, as told in the book of Genesis, but that the divine work of creation goes on at every moment;

God works and labours for me in all creatures upon the face of the earth, that is, he conducts himself as one who labours. Thus, in the heavens, the elements, the plants, the fruits, the cattle, etc., he gives being, conserves them, confers life and sensation, etc. (236)

We can remember how the lilies "neither toil nor spin; yet I tell you, even Solomon in all his glory was not arrayed like one of these" (Matthew 6:28).

This idea has not been absent from the Spiritual Exercises up to this point. Indeed, even in Ignatius' meditations on sin he had a cry of wonder at God's gifts of creation: "And the heavens, sun, moon, stars, and the elements; the fruits, birds, fishes, and other animals – why have they all been at my service!" (60). During the contemplations on the resurrection he recommends that, to help us rejoice in God, we "make use of the light and the pleasures of the seasons, for example, in summer of the refreshing coolness, in the winter of the sun and fire". (229)

God's power is poured out into creation in an unstinting stream of love, not just into inanimate objects, plants, and animals, but into people too. Earlier Ignatius had used the experience of human friendship to help us understand the friendship of Christ: "Consider the office of consoler that Christ our Lord exercises, and compare it with the way in which friends are wont to console each other" (224). Now he takes the idea further and says that all such human virtues flow directly to us from God:

> So, too, justice, goodness, mercy, etc., descend from above as the rays of light descend from the sun, and as the waters flow from their fountains. (237)

With this beautiful image of ongoing movement in the sunlight and in fountains, the Spiritual Exercises draw to a close. Ignatius has given us a key for finding God, not just in meditation on past salvation history, but in all that surrounds us.

God's indwelling

Of all the New Testament writers, perhaps it is John who most powerfully expresses the way God lives in those who reflect the divine goodness:

228

Beloved, let us love one another; for love is of God, and they who love are born of God and know God. . . . Beloved, if God so loved us, we also ought to love one another. No one has ever seen God; if we love one another, God abides in us and his love is perfected in us. (1 John 4:7, 11–12)

Meister Eckhart, a great Dominican mystic of the early fourteenth century, expressed the idea of God's indwelling like this:

If this birth really happens, no creature can hinder you, all point you to God and this birth. . . . No matter what you see and hear, you receive nothing but this birth in anything. All things are simply God to you, who see only God in all things. . . . If this is lacking, this looking for and seeing God in all and sundry, then you lack this birth.

(Sermon on *The Eternal Birth*)

"To grasp God in all things . . .", said Eckhart. "To find God in all things . . .", said Ignatius. He was instructing one of his companions on what answer to give to a Spanish novice master who had asked about prayer and meditation. The reply was that Ignatius

rather approves the effort to find God in all things than that one should spend a long time in prayer. (Letter to Urban Fernandes, 1st June 1551)

Ignatius even writes to one Jesuit, who had spoken of his longing to have less work and more time for prayer, that work can bring him closer to God than even prayer can. The tasks that he sees as distractions from God can be not only the equivalent of the union and recollection of uninterrupted contemplation, but even more acceptable to him, proceeding as they do from a more active and vigorous charity.

(Letter to Manuel Godinho, 31st January, 1552)

And again, speaking of those Jesuits who are still studying, Ignatius gives instructions that they

can hardly give themselves to prolonged meditations. Over and above the spiritual exercises assigned . . . they should practise the seeking of God's presence in all things, in their conversations, their walks, in all that they see, taste, hear, understand, in all their actions, since his Divine Majesty is truly in all things by his presence, power, and essence.

(Letter to Anthony Brandao, 1st June 1551)

Of course, Ignatius is not saying we do not need to set aside any time for prayer alone. If we did not have some time devoted just to prayer we would very quickly lose the habit of finding God in all things outside of our prayer time. But what he does mean is that it is not only when we pray that we are close to God. Or another way of putting it is to say that we can pray all the time. *Laborare est orare* – "To work is to pray" – as the famous Benedictine motto says.

Finally, in the Constitutions for the Society of Jesus, Ignatius says that young Jesuits

should often be exhorted to seek God our Lord in all things, stripping off from themselves the love of creatures to the extent that this is possible, in order to turn their love upon the Creator of them, by loving him in all creatures and all of them in him, in conformity with his holy and divine will.

(*Constitutions*, 288)

These texts give us the origins of the term "Finding God in all things", which is the title of this book, as of this chapter. Herbert Alphonso has described the phrase as "the most perfect Ignatian formulation of the true ideal of Jesuit prayer". Though the phrase in that precise form does not occur in the Spiritual Exercises, the idea of it is expressed most fully in the *Contemplatio ad Amorem*.

Another way of saying the same thing – with another phrase that is just as typically Ignatian – is this: the practice of finding God in all things is a form of "contemplation in action". It was Jerome Nadal, friend and confidant of Ignatius, who said (in an annotation of the examen from the *Constitutions*) that the grace of contemplation in action was granted to all who share the inspiration of Ignatian spirituality, following the example of Ignatius:

> Not only did he know this pre-eminent degree of prayer, in itself a great privilege, but it allowed him to see God present in all things and in every action, and it was accompanied by a lively feeling for supernatural reality. He was a contemplative even while in action, or to use his favourite expression, he was able to find God in all things.

Finding God in all things does not mean only finding God in beautiful things. Of course, when we are in the presence of something beautiful, be it a sunset or a relationship of love, we can relate that back to the divine beauty, of which it is a pale reflection. In my earlier book, *Motherhood and God*, I tried to do just that: I reflected from my experience of loving my own children on how much our creator must love us. The same task can be done by anyone, whatever their state of life or their work: there is a distinctive way in which each individual can find God through the details of their life, whether they be a nurse or a businessman, a factory worker or a poet, a celibate or a married person, a parent or a child.

But in the bad and ugly experiences too we can find a way to God. That sounds harder, and yet people often feel closer to God when they are in need. For example, in times of war we can find God in the courage and generosity of those who suffer. In the inner city we can find God in the gaping human need for meaning, that drives people to drugs or to crime as a feeble substitute for what they really want. In the emaciated body of an AIDS sufferer we can find the body of Jesus who suffered for us on the cross. In the pain of a deserted spouse we can find a witness to the endurance of love, that will not die however much we want to kill it off.

When in ways like this we see the love of God poured out into all things, then we are moved to give back to God all we have, especially those things and those people most dear to us. In a continual sequence, as "the waters flow from their fountains", we receive God's gifts, and return them, knowing that we are not impoverished but enriched by the offering. For if God can be found in all things, then there is nothing at all that can happen to us that we need fear.

For I am sure that neither death, nor life, nor angels, nor principalities, nor things present, nor things to come, nor powers, nor height, nor depth, nor anything else in all creation, will be able to separate us from the love of God in Christ Jesus our Lord. (Romans 8:38–9)

Index to the *Spiritual Exercises*

Paragraphs of the *Spiritual Exercises*	page of this book
2	49, 51
3	28, 83
4	141
5	45
6	190
10	139, 195
12	46
13	184, 187
14	214
15	53
16	42
17	140
18	38, 146
19	30
20	30
21	39, 202
22	51
23	17, 19, 20, 32, 38
24–31	157
44	146
45	28
46	19
45–54	149
46	19
47	72
48	74, 154
50	28
53	29, 143
54	84
55	74, 154
58	152
59	152
60	153, 228

61	154
63	86, 154
69–70	79
71	140
73	58
74	107
75	26
76	23, 64
77	130
83–5	147
86	149
87	147
88	63
89	131
91	73
91–8	107, 175
95	175
98	176
101	64
102	70
103	70
104	74, 168
109	86, 168
111	69, 70
112	71
114	112
114–16	81
116	168
118	137
121–6	113
124	102, 105
125	116
127	66
129	140
131	68
133	140
136–48	107
142	108
146	109
147	85, 86
152	36
154	38
159	116

162	140
165	37, 173
166	37, 173
167	167, 173
169	201, 207
175	212
176	212
177	212
178	212
178–88	212
179	212
180	212
179	19, 40, 42, 207
180	207
181–3	79
183	211
184	213
185	213
186	213
187	213
189	202, 203, 204
192	72
193	74, 146
195–7	79
199	84, 86
202	71
203	74, 171
205	140
209	140
211	148
220	72
221	74, 171
224	228
227	116, 138
229	171, 228
230	202, 225
231	225
232	73
233	74
234	222, 226
235	227
236	227
237	79, 228

238–48	158
249–57	92
250–2	96
252	91
253	96
254	96
257	91
258–60	96
261–312	79, 94
276	80
313–36	181
314	182
316–17	177
318	181, 188
320	187
321	184
322	185
323	184
324	184
328–36	194
330	198
332	195
333	150, 195
334	196
335	136, 182
336	198, 199
337–44	204
338–41	212
338	213
339	213
340	213
341	213
344	204
345–51	196
349	197
351	197
352–70	205
352	205
354	146

General Index

à Kempis, Thomas, 78
Aelred of Rievaulx, 224
affectivity, 223
agere contra, 42–3, 86
Alms, Rules for the Distribution of, 204
Alphonso, Herbert, 224, 231
Alternative Service Book, 90, 145
Anima Christi, see "Soul of Christ . . ."
annotation 19, *see* nineteenth annotation
anointing at Bethany, 123–6
Anthony of Padua, 116
application of the senses, 81
Augustine, 18, 33–5, 95, 116–18, 142, 204
Autobiography of St Ignatius Loyola, 180
awareness exercises, 24–5, Chapter 7

Beckett, Wendy Mary, 102
Benedict, St, 92, 94
Benedictines, 92, 93, 97, 230
Bernard, St, 197
Bible, *passim*
body, use of, 23–7, 147
breathing, 24, 96
Bridget of Sweden, 203

Camaldolese, 220
Cana, marriage at, 119–22
Carthage, Third Council of, 204
Cassian, John, 97
Cassidy, Sheila, 60–1

Catherine of Siena, 203
centring prayer, 25
choice, *see* Election; decision-making
Cistercians, 218–20
Cloud of Unknowing, 97, 103
colloquy, 64, 79, 82–6, 151, 168
communal discernment, 214–17
composition of place, 70–4
confession, 10, 35, 142, 145–6
confirmation of decision, 210–11, 213, 217
consolation, 84, 134, 137, Chapters 10 & 11
  c. without preceding cause, 198–200, 212
Constitutions, 230, 231
Contemplatio ad Amorem, 104, 139–40, Chapter 12
contemplation, 81–2, Chapter 6
  c. in action, 231
contrition *see* repentance
corpse, meditation on, 110, 152
Coudenhove, Ida, 21, 44, 46
creation-centred spirituality, 21

dark night of soul, 186
de Mello, Anthony, 24–5, 60, 70, 92, 109–10, 223
de Saint-Exupéry, Antoine, 179
deception, 193–200
decision-making, 188–9, Chapter 11
desolation, 134, 137, Chapters 10 & 11
detachment, *see* indifference

direction, *see* spiritual direction
discernment, Chapters 10 & 11, *see also* Rules for the Discernment of Spirits
distractions, 192–3
Dominic, St, 149
dryness, 189–92

Eckhart, Meister, 229
Election, 140, 202
"Eternal Lord of All Things . . .", 46, 176
Eucharist, 170–1, *see also* liturgy
examination of conscience (or consciousness), 34, 131, 142, Chapter 8, *see also* general examen; particular examen

fasting, 147–8
First Method of Prayer, 158
First Principle and Foundation, Chapters 1 & 2, 68, 130, 225
First Time for making a decision, 212
First Way of making a decision, 212–13
First Week, 139
Foundation, *see* First Principle and Foundation
Fourth Week, 139–40
Francis of Assisi, 199, 203
Futrell, John Carroll, 180–1

general confession, 10, 146
general examen, 160–6
generosity, 44–8, 175
Godspell, 77
grace, 187
    praying for g., 74–5, 68, 147, 150, 168

"Hail Mary . . .", 85, 88, 96
healing painful memories, 110

hell, exercise on, 81
Hinduism, 97
Hopkins, Gerard Manley, 13, 56, 101, 102, 186
Hound of Heaven, 39
Hughes, Gerard, 11

id quod volo, 74–9, 131
Ignatius of Loyola, *passim*
Illuminative Way, 139–40, 170, 187
imagination, 70–4, 81, Chapter 6, 179–80
Imitation of Christ, The, 78
indifference, 38–43, 173
    in decision-making, 189, 192, 202, 207–10
intercession, 73, 83, 85
Ivens, Michael, 11

Jesuit Refugee Service statement, 174
Jesuits, 10–13, 175, 176, 214–16, 229–31
Jesus, *passim*
Jesus prayer, 97
John of the Cross, 103, 186–7
journal, 132–6, 142
Julian of Norwich, 48, 95, 116, 226

Kempis, Thomas à, 78
Kingdom exercise, 107, 139, 175–6
Kolvenbach, Peter-Hans, 214, 216

La Storta vision, 174–5
lectio, see reading
liberation, theology of, 173, 201
litany, 73, 97
Little Prince, The, 179
liturgy, 139, 145, 152, 155
"Lord, teach me to be generous . . .", 12, 46, 176

Lord's Prayer, *see* "Our Father . . ."
love, 21–2, 46–8, 97, Chapter 9, 202, 213–14, Chapter 12
Ludolph of Saxony, 224

magis, 36
Main, John, 97
mandala, 73
mantra, 73, 97
Mary, 114, 199, 224
  praying to, 85–6, 88, 122
  in mysteries, 70, 71, 72, 115, 119–22, 169
Mary Magdalene, 78–9, 115
meditation, 81–2, *see also* Chapter 5
  m. on corpse, 110
Medjugorje, 199
Mello, Anthony de, *see* de Mello, Anthony
Merton, Thomas, 217–21
Methods of Prayer, *see* First Method of Prayer; Second Method of Prayer; Third Method of Prayer
Mission, The, 12, 176
mission charge, 127–9
Montmartre, vows at, 10, 216
Montserrat, vigil at, 10
mortification, 32, 47
Myers-Briggs workshop, 197
mystery, 69–70, 94, 138, 167–72

Nadal, Jerome, 231
Nicholas Flue, 32
nineteenth annotation, 30, 141

Ochs, Robert, 112
option for the poor, 172–6
oratio, Chapter 5
Othello, 153–4
"Our Father . . .", 26, 44, 89
  at end of prayer, 84, 85, 86–7, 166

  in Second Method of Prayer, 91, 96

Pamplona, siege of, 9, 179
particular examen, 157
Pascal, Blaise, 17, 224
passion, 140, 146, 148, 157, 170–1, 191
penance, 47, 144, 146–9, 187
perseverance, 46
petition, 74, 87
poetry, 95, 134, *see also* Hopkins, Gerard Manley
points, 64–5, 79–82
Polanco, John de, 149
position, bodily, 23–7, 68
poverty, 86, 108–9, *see also* option for the poor
praise, 93, 223
prayer, *passim*
preferential option for the poor, 172–6
Preludes, 64–5, 69–79, 84, 107–8, 135
preparatory prayer, 19, 64–5, 68–9
Presupposition, 51
psalter, 97–8
Purgative Way, 139–40, 170, 187

quiet, prayer of, 29

Radcliffe, Timothy, 20
Rahner, Karl, 102
reading, 66–7, Chapter 5
repentance, 139–41, Chapter 8
repetition, 137–8
resurrection, 140, 170–1, 228
retreat-giver, 51–3, 140–1, 188 *see also* spiritual direction
retreats, 11, 15, 141, 188
  nineteenth annotation r., 30, 141
review, 34, 87, Chapter 7, 190
Richard, St, 77

Rolle, Richard, 33, 223–4
Rules for the Discernment of Spirits, 181, 194–9, *see also* discernment
Rules for the Distribution of Alms, 204
Rules for Thinking with the Church, 205

Sadhana, 24–5, 60, 70, 92, 109–10, 132, 223
St Beuno's retreat house, 11
Saint-Exupéry, Antoine de, 179
Scruples, some Notes concerning, 196–7
Second Method of Prayer, 91, 92, 96
Second Time for making a decision, 212
Second Way of making a decision, 213
Second Week, 139–40
senses, application of, 81, Chapter 6, 138
sequela Christi, 78
simple regard, prayer of, 81
sin, 139–41, Chapter 8, 228
Society of Jesus, *see* Jesuits
"Soul of Christ . . .", 17, 85, 88–9, 96
spiritual direction, 11, 51–3, 140–2, 178, 190, *see also* retreat-giver
Spiritual Exercises, *passim*
spiritual journal, 132–6
spiritual reading, *see* reading
statue exercise, 110

T'ai Chi Ch'uan, 26
"Take and Receive . . .", 46, 222
Teresa of Avila, 103, 186–7
Teresa of Lisieux, 219
thanksgiving, 83, 161, 162, 165, 221
Thinking with the Church, Rules for, 205
Third Method of Prayer, 96–7
Third Time for making a decision, 212–13
Third Week, 139–40
Thompson, Francis, 39
Three Classes of Person, 38–9
Three Degrees of Humility, 37, 173–4
Three Methods of Prayer, 91, 92, 96–7, 158
Times for making a decision, 212–13
tongues, praying in, 63
Transcendental Meditation, 97
Trappists, 218–20
triple colloquy, 85–6
Two Standards exercise, 79, 107–9

Unitive Way, 139–40, 170–1, 187

Vatican Council II, 10

Ward, Mary, 36, 186, 226–7
Ways, Purgative, Illuminative and Unitive, 139

Yarnold, Edward, 27